A Treasury of
TRIVIA

A Treasury of

TRIVIA

Compiled by

DENVER P. TARLE

A HART BOOK

GALAHAD BOOKS

PUBLISHED BY A & W PUBLISHERS, INC.
95 MADISON AVENUE
NEW YORK, NEW YORK 10016

LIBRARY OF CONGRESS CATALOG CARD NO. 81-80066

ISBN: 0-88365-493-8

MANUFACTURED IN THE UNITED STATES OF AMERICA

A Treasury of
TRIVIA

You've dreamed of making a fortune and not paying tax on it, right?

In 1971 Frank McNulty bought an Irish Sweepstakes ticket. The horse was Bronze Hill, and he won. Mr. McNulty went to Dublin and collected $128,410 in winnings. He put the money in a bank on the British island of Jersey.

However, the U.S. Revenue Service demanded that Mr. McNulty pay taxes on his winnings. Mr. McNulty refused, saying he had earned and kept the money outside the U.S. So he was charged with income tax evasion, and sentenced He has spent some four years in jail, but continues to refuse to pay up. Finally, Federal Judge Alfonso Zirpoli has decided that there is no longer any point in keeping McNulty incarcerated. But the chances of his ever enjoying the use of his money are pretty slim—he can't bring it in here, and he will undoubtedly be denied a passport to go there. His winnings are now worth about $140,000, and his tax bill about $70,000. Like the man said: pay the $2!

Among mammals, only men and monkeys are capable of distinguishing colors.

You complain that you never go anywhere? Well, many small rodents live out their entire existence without ever straying more than 20 feet from the place of their birth. On the other hand, a humpback whale often covers more than 4,000 miles in a single year.

A Car in Every Garage

Preceding Henry Ford by two years, Ransom Olds commercially produced a three-horse-power Oldsmobile. He produced over 400 cars a year before the turn of the century.

Henry Ford's ideas were as brilliant from the standpoint of marketing as they were from the standpoint of mechanics. Ford perceived the need to transform the automobile from a luxury to a necessity by making cars cheap and making them simple to operate. His was a car everyone could afford. In its heydey, the flivver sold for about $400. Ford's concept succeeded beyond his wildest dreams, and the Tin Lizzie transformed the face of America. Its success enabled Ford to retire at an early age, whereupon he took up sailing to avoid the traffic jams he had created.

The largest litter ever thrown was 23, by a fox-hound called Lena, on February 11, 1945.

A baby rattlesnake at birth has the same amount of poisonous venom as a full-grown rattler.

Ocean waves are sometimes 80 feet high. Most so-called mountainous waves are only 30 to 40 feet high, and no ocean wave is higher than 100 feet from trough to crest. The highest wave ever scientifically measured was 80 feet tall. But mariners are sure some waves are as high as a ten-story building.

Gasoline has no definite freezing point. Ordinary gas will solidify only under temperatures of between 180 and 240 degrees below zero—a temperature which has never been reached on this planet outside the laboratory.

Fish can be caught in the Sahara Desert. Strangely enough, there are many underground streams in the Sahara—where, by digging through the sand, a desert angler can obtain fresh-water fish.

Birmingham, England—an inland city—has more miles of canals than Venice, the "Queen of the Seas."

You probably know that a female fox is a *vixen*, and a female peacock is a *peahen*, but how about a female aviator? She's called an *aviatrix*. And a female sultan is a *sultana*, a female maharaja is a *maharanee*, a female kaiser is a *kaiserin*, and a female cob (swan) is a *pen*.

A French magazine conducted a survey to investigate sexual behavior in France. If the responses of those interviewed are to be believed, the average Frenchman sleeps with 11.8 women in his life, while the average Frenchwoman shares her bed with only 1.8 men.

Progress is not always without its drawbacks. In 1879, when the first electric arc lights to be used in America for public street lighting were installed in Cleveland, Ohio, many women of that city bitterly complained that the "dazzling white light" showed their complexions to disadvantage.

The longest poem ever penned by one man is the *Shah Namah*, written by the Persian poet Firdausi in the 10th century. The poem, known as "The Book of Kings," is 2,804 pages long, and its 120,000 lines fill nine good-sized volumes. Firdausi worked on the poem for 35 years.

Magnificent Microcosm

Franklin H. Avers of Portage, Wisconsin, made a miniature electric village, which enacts the activities of an average midwestern town from late afternoon to sunrise. This model is mounted on a 5' by 12' stage. As the five-foot curtain opens on the scene, a breeze wafts the scent of flowers out toward the audience and flutters a flag in the park. A motorboat passes a sailboat on the lake, an automobile drives up to a house and honks its horn, and a plane glides in and lands noisily. The sun becomes reddish and finally disappears behind the mountain. Cattle moo, cowbells jingle, the moon appears, stars twinkle. A train pulls into the station, and all is still for a moment to signal the passing of several hours. As the day begins to break, a rooster on a fence crows, the flag is raised, a plane roars, the curtain closes, and the five-minute performance is over.

Just in case you were wondering—the first Eskimo Bible was printed in Copenhagen in 1744.

The largest mushroom farm in the world is located near West Winfield, Pennsylvania, in an old limestone mine. The farm produces about 14 million pounds of mushrooms each year.

It Never Rains, It Pours

New York City, with an average annual rainfall of 43 inches, is pretty bad. Foggy London has only 25, and sunny Los Angeles gets by with 15. Bergen, Norway, seems wet indeed with 73 inches. But Bergen is dry as a desert compared with Cherrapungi, India, which has an annual downpour of 432 inches, or 36 feet!

In 1871, a book entitled *Rosicrucian Dream Book* was published in Boston, containing the solutions to over 3,000 different dream symbols in alphabetical order. According to this work, a dream about potatoes indicates that someone is trying to poison the minds of those who would do you good. And camels in a dream mean that one's beloved is far better than he or she looks.

America's Favorite Hymns

Of the estimated 400,000 Christian hymns that have been published, fewer than 500 are in common use, and only 150 of them are well known by churchgoers. To determine their popularity in this country, a poll was made, not long ago, which disclosed that four hymns alone constituted the first choice of 20,384 of the 30,000 churchgoers questioned. And the relative popularity of these four outstanding favorites is shown by the following figures: For every 100 persons whose first choice was *Abide With Me*, the hymn that led, 75 preferred *Nearer My God to Thee*, 57 preferred *Lead, Kindly Light*, and 47 preferred *Rock of Ages*.

Platinum is so malleable that a troy ounce of the metal can be stretched into a wire more than 10,000 miles long.

The civilized nation with the longest average life expectancy is Sweden—71.6 years for men, 75.4 years for women. These figures just about match those of the Australian Aborigines.

The most spectacular musical event in the United States occurred at the World Peace Jubilee, held in Boston from June 17 to July 4, 1872, to celebrate the end of the Franco-Prussian War. An orchestra of 2,000 instruments, including a bass drum 25 feet in diameter, was bolstered by a chorus of 20,000. To lead this vast aggregation in a rendition of *The Beautiful Danube*, its composer, Johann Strauss, was brought from Vienna at a cost of $20,000—and in 1872, that was quite a sum.

Of all common fowl, the duck is the bird that requires the longest cooking.

In One End, Out the Other

Each day the average person consumes, in one form or another, about three quarts of water. This liquid is released in urine at the rate of about 1/40 ounce per minute, for a total output of 1½ quarts of urine a day.

If the earth were reduced to the size and weight of a ping-pong ball, and the sun shrunk accordingly, Old Sol would still be over 12 feet in diameter and weigh 6,000 pounds. And the sun is one of the smaller stars in our galaxy.

A Welsh rabbit has nothing to do with bunnies. It's a dish made with cheese and beer.

Portuguese explorers journeying to South America brought along convicts on their ships, who were cast ashore in unfamiliar areas to discover if the local natives were cannibals.

An Unabandoned Ship

A drowning swimmer is supposedly done for when he goes down for the third time. Before the Dutch liner *Westerdam* made her first voyage in 1945, she had been sunk three times!

Construction of the boat began in Rotterdam in September, 1939. When the Germans invaded the Netherlands the following year, they seized the ship and set about completing the construction. They had just about finished in 1942, when an Allied bomb sent the *Westerdam* to the bottom for the first time.

German engineers raised the *Westerdam* and began to repair the ship. But Dutch patriots stole aboard, opened the seacocks, and sank her again.

Once more the ship was raised and repaired. This time, Dutch patriots attached explosives to the outside of the hull and sank the ship right next to its pier.

When the war was over, the Dutch raised the *Westerdam* for the last time and rebuilt it as a passenger ship. She was launched in 1945, and became the first passenger vessel to cross the Atlantic after the end of World War II.

What do the terms jeroboam, rehoboam, methuselah, salmanazar, balthazar, and nebuchadnezzar have in common, aside from the fact that each is the name of an ancient king or patriarch? Well, each term also refers to a champagne bottle of a particular size. The jeroboam, the smallest of the six sizes, contains 104 ounces, twice as many as the magnum. The nebuchadnezzar, the largest, contains 520 ounces, or five gallons. And that's an amount of bubbly fit for any king!

The city of Newcastle is the center of England's coal-producing region. So, "to carry coals to Newcastle" means to bring things to a place where they already abound. But an American merchant once accomplished the seemingly absurd feat of shipping coals to Newcastle—and made a handsome profit!

Late in the eighteenth century, a coal miner's strike in Newcastle left the people of that city short of fuel. American merchant Timothy Dexter sent a shipload of coal to Newcastle and easily sold his cargo to the fuel-starved people.

Among his many claims to fame, Benjamin Franklin can list the honor of being the first spelling reform advocate in the United States. In 1768, Franklin proposed a scheme to reform English spelling with a new alphabet. He advocated dropping the letters *c, j, q, w, x,* and *y,* and substituting six new characters, so that every sound in the language could be expressed with one letter.

It is about ten times as easy to shoot a hole-in-one in golf than it is to roll a perfect 300 game in bowling. The odds against the bowler are about 300,000 to 1, while the golfer "enjoys" odds of 30,000 to 1.

Jumping for Joy

One leap from an airplane is about all anyone but a dedicated skydiver would want—literally—to stomach. But on July 5, 1952, Neil Stewart of Birmingham, Alabama, achieved an unenviable record by jumping from a plane 124 times in a single day!

On his first jump, Stewart's parachute failed to open and he had to use an emergency shute. His wife, observing from *terra firma*, fainted. But even that inauspicious beginning did not deter the Alabama jumper. Though once knocked unconscious by a hard landing, Neil jumped 123 more times from the airplane—including 49 jumps in total darkness!

During the early 18th century, Europeans began to hide their latrines inside pieces of furniture. A common custom of the time was to cover the lid of a latrine with a pile of dummy books. To correctly identify the apparatus they shielded, the dummy books always bore the title of *Voyage au Pays Bas*—which means *Journey to the Low Country*—or *Mystères de Paris*.

When you're stuck on a crowded highway it may seem as if everyone and his brother owned a car. Actually, more than half of the people in the world still rely on their own or their animals' muscles not only for transportation, but for all their other power as well.

The hummingbird is the only bird that can fly backwards or hover in the same spot like a helicopter.

When the Wright Brothers made aviation history at Kitty Hawk, North Carolina, their initial 12-second flight spanned a distance shorter than the wingspan of a Boeing 747 jumbo jet—which measures 195.7 feet from tip to tip.

The longest national anthem is that of Greece, which contains 158 verses. The shortest are those of Japan, Jordan, and San Marino, each of which contains but four lines. And the anthems of Bahrain and Qatar contain no words at all.

What could be drier than a desert? Answer: The town of Arica, on the border between Chile and Peru. With a population of 14,000 inhabitants, Arica receives a mere .02 inches of rain per year. This is all the more remarkable because Arica is situated on the Pacific Ocean. To give you an idea of how dry this town is, the rainfall of Arizona—the driest of the 50 American states—is almost 400 times as heavy.

The U.S. Army Overland Train, the longest vehicle in the world, is 572 feet long—almost ⅒ of a mile! The train, which is used to transport rockets or other very long objects, weighs 450 tons, has 54 wheels, 4 engines, and a 7,828-gallon fuel capacity.

The term "limited" when used to refer to an express train does not, as often supposed, refer to the limited number of stops the express will make. Instead, it originates from the practice of running special fast trains with limited seating space.

Texans in a spinach-growing area in the eastern part of the state have erected a statue of Popeye in tribute to his appetite for the vegetable.

Uncurrent Currency

In the early days of our nation, English, French, and Spanish monies all circulated through the American colonies, with a concomitant confusion of trade. In 1785, the dollar was adopted by Congress as a unit of exchange, and the decimal system as the method of reckoning. The U.S. monetary system was established in 1792; the first mint began operation in Philadelphia the following year.

Many coins and bill denominations have come and gone since then. Among the coins no longer in use are the half-cent, the two-cent, the three-cent, the 20-cent, and the silver half-dime. The nickel was not introduced until 1886. Today, gold coins are no longer minted, and you may be surprised to learn that no bills larger than $100 are now placed in circulation.

Spuds, a la France

France was the last European nation to accept the potato. A soldier who had spent considerable time in Germany returned to his homeland to convince fellow Frenchmen that the potato was both edible and delicious, despite medical advice that the vegetable was "toxic and the cause of many illnesses."

Since then, the French have contributed many dishes to the world of potato cookery. One of those dishes, the heralded *pomme soufflées*, has been attributed to a number of chefs.

According to one tale, a 19th-century French chef was charged with preparing a banquet to celebrate the opening of a new railroad line. While preparing the repast at one of the new stations, the chef was notified that the train carrying a coachload of dignitaries to the banquet would be delayed. So he took his half-cooked french fries out of the oil and began preparing a fresh batch. Then he was notified that the train was pulling into the station, on time after all. Frantic, the chef plunged the half-cooked potatoes back into the fat, and the soggy fries puffed into crisp ovals—*pommes soufflées!*

In 1912, George Sewell leapt from an airplane with 12 parachutes harnessed to his body. He opened the first chute, then cut it loose, opened the second chute, and so on, until he'd opened and cut loose 11 parachutes. The 12th chute took him safety to earth.

The Biggest Bloom

If you were to come upon a krubi during a visit to a botanical garden, you might think you were viewing a plant specimen from Jonathan Swift's land of the Brobdingnagians. This flower, a relative of the popular philodendron, is so gigantic that even if you were to stand on another person's shoulder, you would barely be able to reach the top!

The krubi grows in the jungles of Sumatra, a large Indonesian island. Specimens of the krubi have been found to reach the height of 15 feet. The leaves of a well-grown specimen, when unfolded, can cover an area 45 feet in circumference.

But the krubi cannot be termed the largest flower in the world, for it is a collection of flowers simulating a single giant flower.

Mozart, perhaps the greatest pure genius the musical world has ever known, played the harpsichord at age three, composed his first minuet at age five, wrote his first sonata at age seven, and his first complete symphony at age eight! Thereafter, Mozart wrote at least one symphony each year, and eventually produced some 600 symphonies, operas, operettas, concertos, string quartets, sonatas, masses, and other classical pieces.

Mozart was fortunate to have begun his composing career at such a young age, for he died at the incredibly young age of 35!

The game of volleyball is today played around the world, and volleyball competitions have been part of the Olympic Games since 1964. But despite its current global popularity, the game is not an old sport of European vintage. Volleyball was invented in 1895, by a Y.M.C.A. director in Holyoke, Massachusetts. Originally, the game was conceived as a less taxing alternative to the then new game of basketball. By the middle of this century, volleyball was the leading participant sport in the world after golf.

Aviation pioneer Wilbur Wright wrote that the airplane would make war impossible, since air observation could expose an army's movements. In 1911, the Italians demonstrated the first use of aircraft equipped with bombs during the Italo-Turkish War in North Africa.

There was not a single grapefruit growing on the mainland of North America until early in the 19th century. Today, the state of Florida produces 70 percent of all the world's grapefruits.

European governments have always found playing cards an ideal subject for heavy taxation. England began taxing card imports in 1615. By 1628, the tax on each deck had risen to a then exorbitant half-crown. Taxes on playing cards once became so high in Austria that card makers began selling oversized decks that could be gradually trimmed as their edges became worn, thus lasting two or three times as long as a regular deck.

The mass entertainment spectacles of ancient Rome included not only gladiatorial contests, but fights between animals, or between animals and men. When the Roman consul Pompey opened a new theater in 55 B.C., he christened the structure with a show that cost the lives of 500 lions and perhaps 20 elephants. On the inaugural day of the Roman Colosseum in 80 A.D., some 5,000 animals were slain in the arena.

A few years back a woman in Texas loved her dog so much she married him in a standard religious ceremony presided over by a cleric.

The world's first crossword puzzle appeared in the December 21, 1913 edition of the New York *World*. Devised by editor Arthur Wynne, the crossword contained 32 words, in a diamond-shaped diagram with a diamond-shaped opening in the center, and no black squares. Clues were keyed to the diagram by the number of the last square each corresponding answer filled, as well as by the first, as is the case with today's crosswords.

How short was Pepin the Short? The Frankish king, who ruled from 751 to 768, measured just four-and-a-half feet from crown to toe. His sword, when held at his side, stood a foot-and-a-half higher.

Big Wheel

The largest wheels of Swiss Cheese, or Emmentaler, can weigh as much as 220 pounds. A giant Swiss wheel can require over a ton of milk!

Gourmets who savor "authentic" Chinese food may be disheartened to learn that when chop suey was first concocted in New York in 1896, the dish was completely unknown in China. A chef of the Chinese Ambassador Li Hung-Chang devised the dish to appeal to both American and Oriental tastes.

In medieval England, a criminal was punished less severely if he could read and write. A literate criminal could pass under the jurisdiction of the ecclesiastical courts instead of the civil courts; in the church courts, the death penalty could not be handed out for minor offenses. The opening words of the first verse of Psalm 51, which comprised the reading test given to law-breakers, became known as the "neck-verse," for reasons that should be obvious.

In 1486, a law was enacted in England stipulating that every layman convicted of a felony by an ecclesiastical court should be branded on the thumb. The thumb mark barred the felon from receiving "the benefit of clergy," or trial by church court, a second time.

Apples, Apples Everywhere

Johnny Appleseed was a legendary figure, right? Wrong. Johnny Appleseed indeed lived. His real name was Jonathan Chapman, and he was born in Springfield, Massachusetts. Before he died in 1845, he covered more than 100,000 square miles with apple trees!

As a young man, Johnny set out alone into the unexplored wilderness that is now Ohio, Indiana, and western Pennsylvania, with a sack of apple seeds he'd collected from cider mills in Pennsylvania and New York. Wherever he went he planted apple seeds, so that as the years went by, apple orchards bloomed and provided nourishment to pioneers who settled in or passed through the area. He retraced his paths over and over again to cultivate and prune the trees he'd planted.

Along the way, Johnny drew attention with his eccentric garb—a coffee sack for a shirt and a tin pot for a hat, in which he would cook his meals. The attention was fine with Johnny—he distributed Bibles as well as seeds.

The Icelandic language has remained unchanged since the 12th century.

Of the more than 110 species of mammals that have become extinct in the last 1,900 years, at least 70 percent have died out within the last century. About 600 other mammal species are presently endangered and will also perish unless measures are taken now to preserve them.

Of all man-made structures on earth, the only one that might conceivably be visible from the moon is the Great Wall of China.

Spilling the Beans

Intent on preserving a monopoly, the Dutch forbade taking coffee seedlings from their East Indian plantations. But a dashing young Brazilian officer won the heart of the wife of the governor of Dutch Guiana, a coffee growing colony in South America, and as a token of her affection, she gave him some of the precious beans and cuttings, anticipating Cole Porter by declaring her love thusly: "Take the beans, for you're the cream in my coffee!"

The United States postal system is now by far the largest, handling close to one-half of the world's volume. Americans presently post some 80 billion items each year, or about 410 for each citizen, spending over 1.5 billion dollars annually in postal fees.

On a clear day, you can see forever from a lookout point near Chattanooga, Tennessee. Seven states are visible from this promontory—Tennessee, Alabama, Georgia, South Carolina, North Carolina, Virginia, and Kentucky.

Airships like the blimp and dirigible may not be dead yet. American scientists and industrial executives are now studying the possibility of using these vessels for the hauling of heavy machinery and prefabricated structures. Helicopters can carry no more than a 16-ton load, while the gas-inflated airships could hoist as much as a 60-ton load—at a cost far lower than any other form of transportation!

Royal Shenanigans

In the long history of royalty, only one king is know to have been crowned *before* he was even born. When the Persian King Hormizd II died in 310, Persian magnates killed his eldest son, blinded the second son, and imprisoned the third. The throne was reserved for the unborn child of one of Hormizd's wives. In anticipation of the baby's birth, the royal symbol of Persian sovereignity was placed on the pillow in the cradle of the baby-to-be. Three days later, Shapur II came into the world—already a king. One can only wonder how the Persians could be so certain that the baby would be male.

Shapur II went on to become one of the greatest monarchs of his dynasty, reigning for 69 years—including the three days in which he lay within his mother's womb.

An English highway that runs from London to Exeter boasts the smallest underpass in the world—a tunnel one foot wide which was constructed to permit badgers to get safely to the other side of the road.

A controversy once arose in Wisconsin when a mailman refused to handle a particularly pungent shipment of Limburger cheese, claiming that the smell made him ill. A court decision upheld the right of cheese makers to ship their odoriferous product in the U.S. mails.

Some of the major American motion-picture studios now produce as few as a half-dozen or so films each year. In the Hollywood heyday of 1939, all the film companies in this country together turned out an average of two films per *day*!

The push-button elevator, introduced in 1894, was both more reliable and cheaper to operate than the hand-operated manned elevators you can still find in the moldiest of city buildings. Automatic leveling, which brings the car to rest precisely at floor level, made its debut in 1915, but the cry of "watch your step" will live on forever. By the middle of this century, automation had rendered the elevator operator nearly extinct.

You say you have temperamental house plants? Well, there's one specimen of the plant kingdom that really seems to be quite nervous. The colocasia, an Asian and Polynesian plant noted for the profuse water discharge of its leaves, actually has shivering fits! These violent tremors occur at erratic intervals, shaking the entire plant. As yet, scientists have offered no satisfactory explanation for these strange seizures.

The tusks of some male African elephants eventually become so heavy that their owners must frequently rest them in the forks of trees. The longest African elephant tusk on record was some 11 feet long.

Peanut Odyssey

Although many Americans might guess that the peanut was originally an African product, the peanut is, in fact, a native of tropical South America. Spanish conquistadores exploring the New World found South American Indians eating what many called *cacohuate*, or "earth cocoa."

The goober was gradually transplanted in West Africa as a food and fodder crop. Subsequently, slave traders found that the peanut could provide cheap, nutritious food for Africans being carried across the ocean on slave ships. Eventually, some African peanuts were brought to Virginia and planted for livestock fodder. Thus, the peanut made two transatlantic journeys before becoming a North American crop.

Though a great number of meteorites bombard earth's atmosphere each day, only one person on record has ever been killed by a falling meteorite. It happened in 1887, when a man in India was struck in the head by a falling stone.

High-Rise

The apartment building is not an innovation of the modern era. Large apartment dwellings are actually as old as the hills—the Hills of Rome, that is. As early as the first century B.C., many Roman apartment buildings—called *insulae*, or "islands"—rose to a height of five stories. And they might have risen higher, for the Emperor Augustus set a limit of 70 feet on the height of apartment buildings in the Imperial City, for safety reasons.

In today's tall residences, apartments on the upper floors are deemed the most desirable. But in Rome, the lower floors were preferred. Water supply and sanitation pipes usually did not reach above the first floor.

Heavy Hitter!

Composer/pianist Franz Liszt often attacked his piano so violently that hammers would fly from the carriage and strings snap from the force of his blows. Audiences came to expect such accidents, and felt cheated if Liszt did not break at least one string during a concert performance.

A Corker of a Porker

Despite their undeserved reputation for slovenliness, pigs are among the most intelligent of animals. Scientists in the Soviet Union have taught pigs to respond to up to 44 different commands, and have organized "pig circuses" starring their porcine pupils.

American scientists have been stymied in their attempt to import the umi umi, a tiny pig from French Polynesia, for use in biomedical research. Though the umi umi—whose name means "cuddly" in Polynesian—are said to be perfect for research models, United States regulations prohibit the importation of umi umi from the South Pacific due to a fear that the animals could transmit hoof and mouth disease.

By the way, pigs do not sweat. On hot days, they like to wallow in the mud to lower their skin temperature.

The Royal Society for the Prevention of Accidents erected a display stand at the Institute of Personnel Management Conference in Harrowgate, England. It collapsed.

There's One Born
Every Minute

In the summer of 1824, two retired New Yorkers, named Lozier and DeVoe, perpetrated a wild hoax on their numerous friends. They convinced a crowd that they had obtained the mayor's approval to saw off Manhattan from the mainland, and *turn the island around!*

The purpose of this grand plan was to keep Manhattan's southern end from sinking into the harbor under the weight of the many new buildings. DeVoe and Lozier started immediately to sign up laborers, and to award contracts for food, equipment, and even for a huge anchor to prevent the island from being swept out to sea. After eight weeks of preparation, all those associated with the project were instructed to meet the following Monday morning so they could proceed to the north end of Manhattan where the work was to begin. As instructed, hundreds of workmen plus scores of contractors arrived at the spot. They waited for hours before they learned that Lozier and DeVoe had, for reasons of health, gone on an extended journey.

The Atlantic Ocean was not named, as some people believe, for the legendary lost continent of Atlantis—in fact, the name Atlantis was taken from the name of the ocean which supposedly surrounded it. The second largest of the world's oceans was actually named after the Greek Titan Atlas, who in mythology was forced to hold up the earth on his shoulders. Early references to Atlas depicted him holding up pillars which supported the sky. These pillars were thought to rest in the sea we now call the Atlantic Ocean.

Since the figure of Atlas supporting the heavens was often used on the frontispiece of a volume of maps, we now use the word *atlas* to refer to any collection of maps.

Early this century, the so-called "Indian Whiskey" illegally peddled on Indian Reservations often contained plugs of tobacco to make the Indians sick. The Indians, whiskey salesmen claimed, thought an alcoholic beverage that didn't make them sick was inferior. Much of the Indian Whiskey also contained red pepper for "bite," soap for "head," and strychnine for "kick."

The 10 American states west of the Rockies, excluding California (Oregon, Washington, Idaho, Montana, Nevada, Wyoming, Colorado, Utah, Arizona, and New Mexico) have a combined population significantly less than that of California itself. And if all the approximately 15.5 million people living in these 10 states were crammed into Yosemite National Park in California, the park's population density would still be about half that of New York City.

The fastest regularly produced automobiles now available are the Lamborghini Countach and the Ferrari BB Berlinetta Boxer, both of which can reach speeds of 186 miles per hour.

If price is more important to you than speed, you might want to test-drive a Mercedes 600 Pullman, the most expensive standard car now on the market. One of these six-door beauties will set you back close to $100,000— less your trade-in, of course. And if used cars are your preference, you might be interested in a Rolls-Royce Phantom, once owned by the Queen of the Netherlands, that sold in 1974 for a record $280,000!

Big Shots

The "Old Faithful" Geyser in Yellowstone National Park, Wyoming, sends forth more than 33 million gallons of water daily, enough to provide for the needs of a city of 300,000 people. The eruptions of Old Faithful, the most frequently erupting geyser in the world, last about five minutes, and occur every hour or so.

The height of Old Faithful's spout rarely exceeds 150 feet. But to see the tallest active geyser on earth, you won't have to go very far from Old Faithful. Among the 3,000 geysers and hot springs in Yellowstone National Park is Steamboat Geyser, which erupts at intervals ranging from five days to ten months and has sent its fiery spray as high as 380 feet!

Though the word "pencil" might appear to be a diminutive of "pen," the two words come from entire different roots. "Pen" is derived from the Latin *penna*, "feather," while "pencil" is based on the Latin *penicillus*, "little tail," and was first applied to fine-pointed brushes used for painting.

A Careful Decision

In 1844, when Amos Lovejoy and Francis Pettygrove were laying out a new city in what is now the state of Oregon, they could agree upon everything but the choice of a name for their embryonic town. Lovejoy, a Massachusetts native, opted for Boston; Pettygrove, a former Maine resident, held out for Portland. So, the two men did the sensible thing: they flipped a coin. Pettygrove won— and the city was named Portland forevermore.

The fastest speed at which a giant tortoise can crawl is about five yards a minute. A rabbit can cover the same distance in less than a half-second.

By law, the term "Roquefort" may be applied only to cheeses ripened in the damp limestone caves near Roquefort in southeastern France. As long ago as 1411, Charles VI decreed that the term could not be applied to "bastard cheeses made in bastard caves.

Horse Sense

A cavalry troop once captured an entire naval fleet. Sound impossible? Well, the capture had nothing to do with the swimming abilities of the cavalry's horses. Here's how it happened:

In the winter of 1794, French General Charles Pichegru, while fighting the British and Austrians, struck deep into the Netherlands. General Pichegru had invaded Holland during the cold weather months because his troops could easily cross rivers and canals frozen over with thick ice. On January 20, 1795, French soldiers entered Amsterdam and learned that the Dutch fleet was frozen solid in the harbor ice. A cavalry troop of French hussars then rode out onto the ice and captured the entire fleet!

A Bevy of Terms

The English language was once rich with collective nouns to designate groups of animals. The most colorful terms, some of which are still in use, include: a *cete* of badgers; a *muster* of peacocks; an *exaltation* of larks; a *mute* of hounds; a *nye* of pheasants; a *skein* of ducks; a *pride* of lions; and a *skulk* of foxes.

As red as a lobster may be a cliche, but uncooked lobsters are actually dark blue or green in color. The lobster turns red or orange only when cooked.

The fattest man who ever lived, Robert Earl Hughes of Fish Hook, Illinois, weighed 1,069 pounds in the last year of his life. Hughes' waist measurement at that time was 124 inches. When he died in 1958, he was buried in a coffin made from a piano case and transported to the cemetery by a moving van.

Christopher Columbus, the "Discoverer of America," never reached our country. In all, the explorer made four voyages to the New World. On his first two voyages, he landed on islands in the West Indies; on his third trip, he reached South America; and on his fourth voyage, he landed in Central America. But Columbus never set foot on the mainland of North America.

The fastest bird alive is called—appropriately enough—the swift. This speedster is capable of speeds of more than 200 miles per hour.

The Buddhist saint, Dengyo Daishi, crossed the sea to Japan in 805 A.D. and planted tea seeds in a temple garden. The plants flourished. In 815 A.D., the Japanese Emperor, Saga, was entertained at a monastery. He liked the tea so well he decreed that the plants be cultivated in the provinces near his capital. By the 10th century, Japan was growing her own tea instead of importing it from China.

The word *potpourri*, meaning a mixture or miscellany, originally meant simply a stew. The exact translation of the French *pot pourri* is "putrid pot."

When the first mail steamer from the East Coast arrived in San Francisco in 1848, the entire crew deserted to join the burgeoning California gold rush.

A little-known invention by Thomas A. Edison is a doll that talked, the first ever to do so. Built in 1888, the doll had a small phonograph in its body that enabled it to recite a dozen nursery rhymes. After making several hundred of these dolls, Edison was informed that his company had previously sold the right to manufacture phonograph toys to another firm. Although that firm had never exercised its right, Edison stopped production and had the dolls destroyed. Of the few he saved and presented to friends, only two are believed to be in existence today.

Four men in the history of boxing have been knocked out in only 11 seconds of the first round.

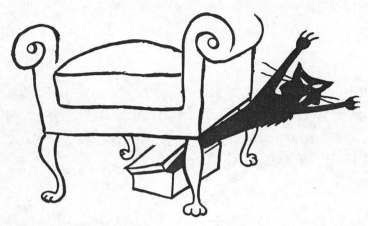

Cat on Cue

David Belasco's 1879 play *Hearts of Oak* began with a cat walking out from under an armchair and stretching before a log fire. Theatre-goers were puzzled as to how the animal could be taught such perfect timing. Months later, Belasco revealed that before curtain time each night, the cat was squeezed into a box hidden under the chair and, as the curtain rose, released from its temporary prison by means of an offstage cord. The cat then naturally crawled out and stretched its cramped muscles.

In 1874, the first practical typewriter was placed on sale by E. Remington and Sons. You might imagine that the first Remingtons were scooped up by clever businessmen as fast as they could be manufactured. Not true. Most businessmen couldn't see the advantage of a machine only slightly faster than handwriting that cost, in the words of one, "a thousand times as much as a pen." As late as 1881, Remington was selling only 1,200 machines a year.

Contrary to popular opinion, a lightning bolt does not move at the speed of light. Most downward bolts do not reach speeds over 1,000 miles per second, though the upward return stroke that follows most downward bolts can reach speeds of up to 87,000 miles per second, nearly half the speed of light.

The common length of a lightning bolt is about half a mile, although bolts may be as short as 300 feet or as long as five miles. In rare instances, a lightning bolt may stretch up to 20 miles. No matter the length, a single flash of lightning can carry as much as 100 million volts of electricity.

The wood sorrel, a flowering plant widely distributed throughout the North temperate regions, will droop heavily if a leaf is touched—or even breathed upon. What is amazing about the wood sorrel is that an impulse is transmitted almost immediately throughout the plant from the one touched leaf. Thus, if one raindrop falls on one leaf, the plant will fold and droop at once. Experiments have shown that the wood sorrel is so sensitive that it will fold up and droop even at the vibration of approaching footsteps!

The longest completed chess match on record, to date, took place in Baku, U.S.S.R., in 1945. The match—which ended in a draw—took 21½ hours and consisted of 171 moves.

Three presidents of the United States—Thomas Jefferson, John Adams, and James Monroe—died on July Fourth. Jefferson and Adams died on the very same day, in 1826.

Yellow Press

The newspaper comic strip in the United States was born out of the rivalry between two giants of the American press. In 1893, the *New York World* published the first full-color comic page in the nation, depicting a set of humorous characters under the title *Hogan's Alley*. Soon afterward, publisher William Randolph Hearst countered with the first weekly full-color comic supplement, eight pages in the *Morning Journal*.

Hearst's supplement featured *Yellow Kid*, a strip by Richard Outcault, whom Hearst had lured away from the *World*. *Yellow Kid* was the first continuous comic character in the United States, and standardized the use of speech balloons for comic strip dialogue.

Incidentally, the Italian word for comic strip is *fumetto*, "little puff of smoke," so-named after the speech balloon.

Bolts from the Blue

How frequently does lightning occur? World-wide, over 100 lightning flashes occur each *second!* In the United States alone, about 400 persons are killed and 1,000 injured by lightning each year. But lightning takes its biggest toll on trees. Each year, about 7,000 forest fires in the United States are caused by lightning, resulting in the destruction of perhaps millions of trees.

Still, your chances of being struck by lightning in your lifetime have been estimated to be more than a million to one. A morbid fear of lightning, called keraunophobia, is thus quite without foundation—and quite useless. For if you see the lightning, it missed you; and if it does strike you, you won't know it!

The ancient city of Babylon's most important street, often called the Processional Way, was actually named "The Street on Which May No Enemy Ever Tread." Alas, many a foe came to tread on Main Street, Babylon, before the city was razed to the ground.

Bizarre Botanica

If you've ever walked into a butcher shop where sausage links and salamis dangled from the ceiling, you have an idea of what it might be like to stand under a spreading sausage tree. Surely one of the oddest looking plants on earth, this African native grows to a height of 30 to 40 feet. Its large hanging flowers bloom at night, giving off a mouselike odor that is appealing to the tree's favorite pollinator, the bat. But it is the fruit that gives this tropical wonder its remarkable appearance, and its name.

Cordlike stalks hanging from the branches end in long, slender fruits which greatly resemble sausages. Some grow in bunches like bananas, others dangle alone at the end of their stalks. These wiener-shaped marvels are usually about one to two feet long, but can grow to three feet and can weigh up to 15 pounds each!

Of all mammals, the greyhound shows the greatest disproportion of the sexes—110 male greyhounds are born for every 100 females.

You can't have George Washington to dinner, but you can have dinner in George, Washington. The town of George, which was home for 273 persons at the time of the 1970 census, honors its namesake every July Fourth with a mammoth 1,200-pound cherry pie.

Even that pie might look like a mere fruit tart compared to the largest cherry pie on record, a six-ton pastry colossus baked in Charlevoix, Michigan, to mark the 1976 Bicentennial.

Easy Money

Henry Ford began his motor company in 1903 with capital of only $28,000, 12 workers, and a plant only 50 feet wide. Additional funds were supplied by the Dodge brothers, themselves auto manufacturers. The Dodges' initial $20,000 investment was eventually worth $25 million.

In 1908, preparation for the Model T's production brought Ford so close to bankruptcy that he had to borrow $100 from a colleague's sister to pay for the car's launch. That $100 was eventually worth $260,000 to the generous donor!

An age-old belief holds that the easiest way to assure a rainy day is to leave your umbrella at home. Robert Louis Stevenson seemed aware of this peculiar meteorological wisdom when he wrote: "There is no act in meteorology better established . . . than that the carriage of the umbrella produces dessication of the air; while if it be left at home, aqueous vapor is largely produced, and is soon deposited in the form of rain."

The first commercial telephone switchboard appeared in 1878 in New Haven, Connecticut, linking just 21 phones. The first telephone directory was in the hands of New Haven phone users in 1878—listing only 50 names. And the first pay telephone reared its coin-snatching head in 1889, in Hartford, Connecticut.

In the early 1950s, the average American family paid about 11 percent of its income in taxes. By the mid-70s, the same family paid twice as much in taxes—about 23 percent of its income.

Going Bananas

The banana is now America's favorite fresh fruit. The apple and orange are consumed here in greater numbers, but both fruits are frequently enjoyed in juices and other processed products. Bananas are almost always eaten fresh. Americans now devour over 12 billion bananas each year—close to 19 pounds per person! Yet virtually no bananas are grown within this country—and the fruit was almost unknown here just a century or so ago!

Talk about big spenders! An Indian maharajah who stayed at the Savoy Hotel in London, one of the world's costliest, took 35 rooms, kept 20 limousines at his disposal, and ordered 3,000 fresh roses daily!

A French hotel catering to English-speaking guests once had eggs billed on its menu as "extract of fowl." They were offered both "peached" and "sunside up."

In the years immediately following the Wright Brothers' first airplane flight, most magazine and journal editors regarded the Wrights' story as so much science fiction, refusing to believe that a man had actually flown at Kitty Hawk. Amazingly enough, the first eyewitness account of a Wright Brothers' flight was published in a magazine called *Gleanings in Bee Culture*, after its editor witnessed a flight of the Wrights' second machine, *Flyer II*.

?:".(;/,'!

In 1802, Timothy Dexter, an eccentric American businessman, published a collection of his philosophical musings, entitled *A Pickle for the Knowing*, that boasted a host of unprecedented spellings and a total absence of punctuation!

In a second edition of the book, Dexter made a concession to traditional grammar and included punctuation. But the periods, commas, and other punctuation marks were all lumped together in an appendix, so that readers could "pepper and salt [the book] as they please."

In a sense, the French were the first to depend upon airmail postal delivery for any length of time. During the siege of Paris in the Franco-Prussian War of the 1870s, mail was sent out of the capital by balloon, along with hundreds of homing pigeons. Return letters were photo-reduced to one four- thousandth of their original size, then delivered to the capital by pigeon. Thirty-five pigeons carried the identical 30,000-message mail cannisters so that at least one was certain to survive Prussian pigeon snipers. In Paris, the messages were enlarged on a projection screen, copied by clerks, and delivered to addressees within the city.

The lobster and related shellfish are, in a manner of speaking, "insects of the sea." Lobsters are Anthropods, a phylum which includes the insects, and crustaceans, a class that also includes shrimps and crabs. Crustaceans, like insects, have a horny exoskeleton, jointed appendages, and segmented bodies. In short, if a lobster a half-inch long were crawling across your wall, you'd probably swat it.

The Louisiana Purchase of 1803, which transferred from France to the United States some 100 million acres, including probably the richest agricultural area in the world, cost this nation just $15 million, not including interest payments. Today, a moderate sized parcel of land in Manhattan may sell for more than that amount!

In 1960, the *Journal of the American Medical Association* reported that a patient checking into a hospital for a swollen ankle had been found to have swallowed 258 items—including a 3-pound piece of metal, 26 keys, 39 nail files, and 88 assorted coins.

Bathing, Roman Style

During Imperial times, the Roman's bathing ritual consisted of a series of baths, each taken in a different room of the massive public baths. The bather began in the undressing room, then moved to another room where he was anointed with oil, then to the gym for exercise. After the gym came the *calidarium*, or hot bath; then the steam room; then the *tepidarium*, or lukewarm bath; and finally, the *frigidarium*, or cold bath, which was usually a sort of swimming pool. Sounds much like our modern health spa, doesn't it?

The Roman baths were open continually, except for religious holidays and times of national crisis. Customarily, a Roman would bathe before the principal meal of the day, but some of the more idle—and cleaner—citizens went through the entire bathing ritual as many as six or seven times a day!

If you were standing on Pluto, the most distant planet in our solar system, the sun would appear no larger or brighter in the sky than the brightest star does in our sky.

Many Americans who commute to and from work by automobile must drive for over an hour in each direction. If we take eight hours as the time the average American passes in slumber, we can say that many persons in this country spend up to 15 percent of their waking hours in the confines of their home-away-from-home, the automobile!

Early this century, Philadelphia Athletics owner Connie Mack awarded pitcher Rube Waddell a contract stipulating that Waddell's battery mate, Ossie Shreck, could not eat crackers in bed when the pair shared a room on the road. In those days, players had to share not only a hotel room when traveling, but the same bed as well!

Dave White's round at the Winchester Country Club started fine, but he blew up on the fifth hole and took a horrifying 13! Then the Massachusetts pro settled down with a vengeance. He shot 10 straight birdies to salvage a par round of 72.

In 1918, at Bahia Feliz, Chile, rain fell on all but 18 days of the year. And on those 18 it drizzled!

Rum, obtained from fermented sugarcane or fermented molasses, is produced primarily in the Caribbean. Different varieties derive from Puerto Rico, Cuba, Jamaica, and Mexico.

When a Manchurian child is ready to learn how to walk, his parents often embroider a cat's head, whiskers and all, on the toes of his shoes. The parents hope that this will make their child as sure-footed as the cat.

The fattest man on record was Robert Earl Hughes, who bequeathed over 1,000 pounds of adipose tissue to posterity when he died of uremia in 1958, in Bremen, Indiana. The heaviest woman, Mrs. Percy Pearl Washington, came 150 pounds short of Hughes' record. She weighed about 880 pounds at her death, in 1972, in Milwaukee.

The dog who is reputed to have lived the longest was a black Labrador named "Adjutant," who died on November 30, 1963, at the age of 27 years and three months.

Weather or Not

The first thermometers, devised independently by Galileo and Sanctorius at the turn of the 17th century, consisted essentially of a bulb atop a stem which descended into a liquid. Heating or cooling the bulb affected the height of the column of liquid in the tube, which was marked by a scale.

About a hundred years later, in 1714, Fahrenheit of Danzig invented the mercury thermometer to measure heat. The thermometer of Reaumur, invented about 15 years later, used alcohol to measure cold. Mercury was not feasible for this thermometer because mercury solidifies at -39 °C.

The centigrade thermometer, created by Celsius in 1742, is used primarily in laboratory work. It has the computational advantage of a 100-degree range between the freezing point and the boiling point.

Monkey Business

A Southern psychologist installed two chimpanzees in adjoining cages, and tried to determine how quickly they could distinguish between two different-colored coins. One cage contained a slot machine that dispensed water only after the insertion of a white coin; the other cage contained a machine that dispensed food and worked only with a black coin. On the first day, each chimp was given a bagful of mixed coins, and soon learned which coins worked his machine.

A few days later, the chimp with the water dispenser was deprived of water for 24 hours, and the one with the food dispenser was deprived of food for 24 hours. Then the thirsty monkey was given food coins, and the hungry one water coins. Instead of being baffled by the ploy, the chimps reached through the bars of their cages and exchanged coins with each other.

A tiny tropical fish called the anableps has eyes that work just like a pair of bifocals. The upper half of each eye is focused for water-surface vision, the lower half for underwater sight.

The bow and arrow date from prehistoric times as instruments of survival and weapons of war, but the sport of archery is English in origin. In medieval times, a number of great English military victories were largely due to the skill of English archers, and British monarchs have always encouraged the sport among the populace. Charles II enacted laws in the 17th century to guarantee an ample supply of bows and arrows for all citizens— and other monarchs on occasion forbid the playing of other games, lest they interfere with archery!

Brussels' best-known statue is "le Manikin Pis," a 20-inch figure of a boy responding to Nature's call, that has stood in the heart of the city for 500 years. During this time, personages such as Louis XV and Napoleon have presented the bronze lad with many medals, swords, and fancy uniforms which he has worn on appropriate occasions. Among the costumes have been the dress of a Belgian Grenadier, a French Chevalier, a British Master of Hounds, a Chinese Manchu, an Indian Chief, and an American G.I.

Missouri and Tennessee both touch on eight other states.

The sound of the bagpipe may immediately conjure up the image of Scotsmen in kilts, but the instrument actually predates the Scottish nation. Instruments identical to the bagpipe were played in ancient Persia, Egypt, Chaldea, and Greece. Roman soldiers played the bagpipe as they marched to far corners of the Empire. It was the Romans, in fact, who first brought bagpipes to the British Isles.

The record for non-stop piano playing is 44 days, set by Heinz Arntz in 1967. Except for two hours of sleep each day, the 67-year-old Arntz played continually for 1,056 hours. During his stint, which began in Germany, Arntz was carried in a van to a seaport and traveled from Germany to the United States on a steamship, finishing his performance at Roosevelt, Long Island.

The early kings of France stuck three hairs plucked from their beards in the seal of official papers to lend the documents greater sanction.

To facilitate the printing of horse-racing sheets, regulations insist that the name of a race horse may not contain more than 18 letters, hyphens, apostrophes, and spaces.

Nobody's Perfect

A plaque on the par-five ninth hole of a Los Angeles golf course commemorates the achievement of Arnold Palmer in the 1961 Los Angeles Open. No, Arnie didn't score an ace on that hole, or even a triple birdie. He recorded *12 strokes*, including five out-of-bounds shots!

There are more than 3,000 varieties of tea. Like wines, teas take their names from the districts where they are grown, such as Darjeeling, Assam, Ceylon, etc.

You've certainly heard of the 4-H Club, but did you know what the four H's stand for? Head, Heart, Health, and Hands.

Pasta and tomatoes are today regarded as the most essential elements of Italian cuisine, but neither appeared in Italy before the Renaissance. Pasta originated in China, and may have been first brought to Europe by Marco Polo. Tomatoes are natives of tropical America, and did not reach Europe until the 16th century.

String 'Em Up

The term "lynch," used in this country to designate the unlawful execution of an accused person by mob action, may appear to be a time-worn word of old English vintage. Actually, the term is of recent coinage—and owes its origin to a man's name!

Capt. William Lynch, who died in 1820, organized a vigilance committee in Pittsylvania County, Virginia, to apprehend and punish a band of outlaws. Lynch's method of dealing summarily with thugs gave rise to the expression "Lynch's law," which spawned the verb "lynch."

The city of Lynchburg, Virginia, was named after another Lynch, John, the reputed founder.

Your birthday may not be such a special day after all—you share it with at least nine million others.

A Pane-ful Story

Glass was made in prehistoric times, and glass-making was already a well-established industry in Egypt by the 16th century B.C. The Romans refined the art of glassmaking to a level unequaled until modern times. They made small windowpanes, hollow ware, and colorful millefiori (thousand flowers) vessels.

After the Crusades, Venice was the leader in making fine glassware for almost four centuries. The city officials tried to monopolize the industry by strictly controlling the glassworkers at Murano. Artisans were severely penalized for betraying the secrets of their art.

France became dominant in the 18th century with the invention of a process for casting glass. French plate glass was used to line the magnificent Galerie des Glaces at Versailles.

The first glass manufactory on this side of the Atlantic was built in 1608.

If the amount of soap used is any indication of a nation's cleanliness, the English are the cleanest people in Europe. A recent survey, conducted by a Swiss organization, found that the average Englishman uses 40 ounces of soap each year. Switzerland ranks second with 37 ounces per person, followed by West Germany, France, and the Netherlands.

The four busts of American presidents carved into the side of Mount Rushmore, in South Dakota, average 60 feet from the top of the head to the chin. Abraham Lincoln's mouth alone measures 22 feet in length, and a man could easily stand in Thomas Jefferson's eye. If a full-figure statue of one of the presidents was constructed on the scale of the Mount Rushmore busts, the statue would stand 465 feet tall!

The word *ye* in such expressions as "Ye Olde Shoppe" is pronounced like the word *the*. The letter *y* in Anglo-Saxon indicated the same *th* sound apparent in the current spelling.

There are 30 times as many people buried in the earth as there are people now living.

Packing Them In

The World Championship Sardine Packing Contest is held every year in Rockland, Maine. To pack a sardine, one must pick it up, deftly snip off its head and tail with razor-sharp scissors, and place it neatly in an open sardine can. The all-time record for sardine-packing is held by Mrs. Patricia Havener of Waldoboro, Maine, who in 1971 packed 450 sardines into 90 cans in just 10 minutes.

The card game poker became popular in the United States in the 19th century, especially among gold-digging forty-niners. The game was actually based on an older Spanish game called *primero* that included elements of betting and bluffing just like the modern game. According to Shakespeare, Henry VIII played *primero* the night Queen Elizabeth was born. The term "poker" comes to us from the German *pochen*, "to brag" or "to knock," or from a similar German game called *pochspiel*.

Malaria is the most prevalent infectious disease threatening man. Malarial fever strikes about 300 million people each year throughout the world, resulting in some three million deaths. In India alone, a million deaths a year were attributed to malaria around the middle of this century. In some parts of the world, virtually the entire population is constantly infected with the disease.

Malaria is a worldwide disease, especially prevalent in the tropics. But some tropical areas, such as Hawaii and the Fiji Islands, are malaria-free, due to the absence of the disease-carrying mosquitoes.

American advertisers now spend well over two *billion* dollars each year on television commercials—not including the cost of making the ads themselves. How much money is that? Well, in a recent year, the nations of Ecuador, Sri Lanka, and Kenya each had a Gross National Product of less than three billion dollars.

Shepherds and farmers have been fooled by a monstrous fungus known as the giant puffball. This mushroom-like plant is so large that a specimen growing in the grass of a pasture can, from a distance, be mistaken for a reclining sheep!

The giant puffball is a white, globular-shaped fungus that grows on the ground with no visible stalk. In shape and size it most resembles a human brain; in fact, the puffball is also called the *Tête de Mort*, or Death's Head. But specimens have been found that were close to four feet long and weighed well over 20 pounds.

Incidentally, despite its name the *Tête de Mort* is quite edible. A large specimen could feed an entire family.

Silver Wares

In the late eighth century, Charlemagne sanctioned the abandonment of the gold standard in Western Europe, and established a monetary system based on silver. A silver penny, or *denarius*, was the basic unit, with 240 pennies to a pound of silver. The words *livre*, *lira*, and *pound*, as used in British currency, date from this era. The Pound Sterling was originally 240 sterlings, or silver pennies, and literally weighed one pound.

Gold came back into use during the 13th and 14th centuries, with the *florin*, from Florence, among the more important coins. But the older silver system remained in use, so that, through the Renaissance, two basic monetary systems were current in most of Europe. Financial calculation was indeed a laborious job.

The peak year for American newspapers—in terms of sheer numbers—was 1916, when 2,461 dailies were published across the nation. By 1944, consolidation and bankruptcy had brought that figure down to 1,744.

The vanilla plant is a climbing orchid that attaches itself to trees with aerial rootlets, though the plant does possess ordinary soil roots. Vanilla is unique among the some 20,000 species of orchid known throughout the world, for it is the only orchid that produces a commercially useful commodity.

An airplane once crashed into a New York office building and struck directly into the elevator shaft, destroying the cables. The car plunged 17 floots—but the buffer, a safety device at the bottom of the shaft, saved the life of the elevator's lone passenger!

Since at least the 14th century, the English cutlery industry has been centered around the city of Sheffield. It was 19th-century Sheffield cutlerers who began fitting pocketknives with various other tools, among them buttonhooks, files, leather borers, tweezers, gimlets, saws, and implements curiously known as "castrating blades." One interesting Sheffield creation sported both a pistol and a dagger.

A 19th-century London tavern owner was frightened one evening by a peculiar whistling sound emanating from his storage cellar. Fearing a thief, he tiptoed into the cellar and began gingerly trying to locate the source of the plaintive wailing. What he found was so remarkable that he invited a number of his usual patrons to a special dinner the following night—when Charles Dickens, William Thackeray, and other London notables were delighted by the performance of a singing oyster!

There are more individual species of insects on earth than there are men. Each year about 1,000 new species are discovered.

The noted authors who often worked in bed include Cicero, Horace, Milton, Voltaire, Jonathan Swift, Alexander Pope, Mark Twain, and Marcel Proust. British writer Max Beerbohm once declared that his ideal of happiness was "a four-poster in a field of poppies."

The papyrus reed, or *biblos*, was cultivated in the Nile Delta at least as early as 3,500 B.C. Egypt supplied papyrus for the entire ancient world, for the *biblos* has never been grown in any quantity outside that country. Egyptian papyrus was so vital to the Roman Empire that a papyrus crop failure during the reign of Tiberius nearly brought all official and commercial business in Rome to a complete halt.

The game of badminton was named after the country estate of the English Duke of Beaufort, where the game is thought to have been played for the first time in 1873. But similar games were played earlier in India, and badminton itself was probably developed from the old game of battledore and shuttlecock.

The battledore, the "racket" used to strike the shuttlecock in the early game, probably derived its name from a club used by launderers to beat or smooth clothes.

In 1878, the first American badminton club was formed in New York City, but its charter curiously limited play to men and "good-looking single women."

Great Guns

The invention of firearms in the 14th century did not immediately spell the doom of the armored knight. Most early hand guns were not powerful enough to pierce armor. The crossbow remained in common use until the 16th century, and armor makers continued to flourish into the 17th century.

But early cannons, or "thunder guns," were powerful enough to demolish castle walls, and therefore helped bring about the end of the feudal society in which the armored knight reigned supreme.

Basque farmers in the Pyrenees Mountains use flying saucers to catch pigeons! The birdcatchers wait in mountainside perches for flocks of migrating pigeons, then sail saucer-shaped paddles called *zimbelas* just ahead of the flock. The birds mistake the *zimbelas* for hawks and dive toward earth, only to be caught in huge nets stretched across the valley below. The Basques then ship the pigeons to markets in France, where the birds are considered a delicacy.

What Hit Me?

A big crowd was assembled at the Lewiston, Maine, boxing arena on September 24, 1946, expecting to see a battle royal between Al Coutoure and Ralph Walton. But those spectators who were a few seconds late in taking their seats missed the entire fight. As the bell rang for the first round, Coutoure rushed at Walton 'and swung his trusty right. Walton caught the punch smack on the chin. Including the ten seconds the referee counted over Walton's prostrate figure, the whole fight took only 10½ seconds!

If you think that fight has to be the shortest on record, think again. On September 2, 1957, the bell for the first round rang in Maestag, Wales, and a Nigerian welterweight named Bob Roberts rushed at his English opponent, Teddy Barker. Roberts swung, Barker ducked and came through with a right counter, catching the overenthusiastic Roberts square on the jaw. The Nigerian collapsed, then staggered to his feet. But the referee stopped the bout and awarded Barker the victory on a TKO (technical knock-out).

The entire fight had lasted just seven seconds!

In the 15th century, Portuguese seamen bound for the East Indies brought along umbrellas as fit gifts for native royalty. Upon landing on a strange island, the seamen immediately opened an umbrella over their captain's head, to demonstrate his authority.

Rome XII, Pompeii VI

So football is a relatively new, American game? Actually, games similar to modern football predate the discovery of America!

The ancient Romans played a game called *harpastum* that included many features of modern football and soccer. An inflated animal bladder was probably used for the ball. Here's how a Roman historian described the game: "The players divide themselves into two teams. The ball is placed on a line between them. At the two ends of the field are two other lines, beyond which the two teams strive to carry the ball."

By the eighteenth century, English football was so violent that a French spectator observed: "If Englishmen call this playing, it is impossible to say what they would call fighting."

There is now about one car in this country for every two persons. In contrast, only one person in every 14,500 owns a car in China.

A Concert of Swine

The musical highlight of the Great Exhibition of 1851, in England, was an instrument called the pigtail organ. The organist of this most unusual instrument had assembled a herd of pigs, each of which had a squeal of a different pitch. The tails of the melodic swine were connected to a system of pincers, which were operated by the keys of the organ. To play the instrument, the organist merely pressed the desired keys and—*viola!*—the pigs squealed out a melody, to the delight of the audience.

Down-at-the-mouth telephone users in New York City no longer have to call a friend to hear a few words of good cheer. On April 1, 1974—approximately, April's Fool's Day—the New York Telephone Company instituted a Dial-a-Joke service, offering a new joke each day for the price of one call. On the average, close to a million calls are received by the Dial-a-Joke number each month, with 3,331,638 calls standing as the record for one month.

A Welsh zoologist has been working on a high-protein burger made from rat meat. And other scientists with tainted tastebuds have proposed a burger made from cotton—talk about flannelmouth!

São Paulo, Brazil, is the most populous city south of the equator. The São Paulo metropolitan area presently has a population of over nine million. Demographic experts predict that if São Paulo continues to grow at the present rate, the city's metropolitan area will, by the year 2000, top the 25-million mark!

Parts of the moon have been more thoroughly explored than some regions on earth. Much of the Amazon Basin and parts of Antarctica, Greenland, and Saudi Arabia have never been explored and mapped by civilized man.

Holy Rollers

Dice are the oldest gaming implements known to man. Before dice became gaming pieces, numbered cubes were used as magical devices for divining the future. The next time you're searching for a word to stump a self-proclaimed vocabulary know-it-all, try *astragalomancy*. That's the practice of divination by means of dice!

Archaeologists have shown that dice predate the written word, and can be found in almost every culture in the world. Excavations in Egypt have turned up stone dice dating from 2,000 B.C. Archaeologists in China have discovered gaming cubes from 600 B.C. that look remarkably similar to the modern thing. And dice especially made for cheating have been found in the tombs of Egypt, the Orient, and the Americas!

The Mightiest Midas

The wealthiest monarch of all time was probably Ashurbanipal, King of Assyria, who amassed a fortune equal to *three trillion* dollars before his death in 625 B.C.

Having inherited riches beyond imagination from kings who preceded him on the Assyrian throne, the king added to his riches by conquering Babylonia and Egypt and seizing vast amounts of gold and jewels. The personal wealth of this potentate was so tremendous that if he were alive today—and felt generous enough—he could pick up the tab for the entire United States federal budget for five straight years, and still have about half of his great fortune left!

The Best-kept Secret

Since the invention of Coca-Cola, only seven men have ever known the formula for the drink. Today, only two are living, and as a precaution these two men never fly in the same airplane.

Incidentally, 90 million bottles of Coke are drunk each day throughout the world.

Persons wishing to immigrate to New Zealand must answer a number of questions pertaining to their health, none less weighty than: "Susceptible to bunions?"

If you're eagerly awaiting the day when you open an oyster and find a small pearl inside, don't hold your breath. Pearl oysters are found only in tropical waters, and are not considered fit for consumption.

Key West, Florida, is not the southernmost point in the United States—not since Hawaii became a state, that is. The southernmost point in the nation is now Ka Lae, or South Cape, on the island of Hawaii.

You might think that Reykjavik, Iceland, which lies almost on the Arctic Circle, is one of the coldest capital cities on earth. Actually, Reykjavik has a warmer mean temperature—29 degrees—than Chicago, Detroit, or Boston during January, Reykjavik's coldest month.

Quaking with Fear

In 1886, an earthquake shook Charleston, South Carolina, toppling 1,400 chimneys to the ground in 70 seconds. No buildings in the city were entirely demolished, but more than 50 people died, and damage was estimated at 5 million dollars. The quake was felt as far away as Bermuda.

The greatest earthquakes to strike the United States centered around New Madrid, Missouri, in 1811-1812. The three quakes were felt as far away as Canada, and toppled chimneys in Cincinnati, Ohio—400 miles away!

And in 1935, three earthquakes and almost continual earth tremors kept the residents of Helena, Montana, shaking for a full year—in more ways than one.

The wildcat is the most vicious fighter in the animal kingdom. Asleep, it resembles a gentle housecat—in a fight, it is a furry ball of rage. This spitfire's speed gives it an advantage over most other animals. In one swift leap, it can rip open its enemy's throat with its razor-like teeth.

The Long and the Short of It

The longest name of any city or town in the world belongs to the Welsh city of LlanfairpwllgwynggyllgogerychwyrndrobwellLlantysiliogogogoch. Compare that to the French village of Y, or the Norwegian town A.

The term *bootlegger* originated on the Indian reservations of the West. Since it was unlawful to sell alcoholic spirits to the Indians, ingenious peddlers often carried flasks of firewater in their boots to conceal them from government agents.

The first ferris wheel was erected at the 1893 Columbian Exposition in Chicago. Built by George Ferris, the wheel had 36 cars, each capable of holding 60 passengers, and rose to a height of 264 feet.

In a Nutshell

Early American artists were fond of miniature wood carvings, but in some cases they may have carried their craft a bit too far. The Peabody Museum in Salem, Massachusetts, contains a wood carving done in the inside halves of a rosary bead which depicts, in one half, Judgement Day, and in the other, Heaven. The entire scene in each half is less than 2 cubic inches in area, yet includes close to 50 figures—none of which can be seen without a magnifying glass.

Air-conditioning is good business. Tests have shown that absenteeism is less and efficiency far higher in air-conditioned offices and factories.

A Spooky Hill

Stop your car at the foot of a sloped street in Lake Wales, Florida, set the gears in neutral, release the brake, and watch your car begin to roll—uphill!

The slope, known as Spook Hill, has puzzled tourists and residents alike for many years. Oranges and grapefruits dropped on the street at the foot of the slope roll uphill. Liquid poured on the street seems to flow upwards. Engineers with tripods and levels try to measure the slope, and walk away shaking their heads.

"It's an optical illusion," said a Lake Wales City Manager, but he refused to tell just how the illusion of Spook Hill works.

The well-known Saratoga potato chips were invented, not surprisingly, in Saratoga, New York, when a guesthouse chef, appropriately named George Crumb, lost his patience with a guest who insisted on thin french fries. Crumb cut a potato into paper-thin slices, dropped them in oil, and—presto!—another American institution was founded.

An inn in Soleure, Switzerland, called the *Krone*, still possesses a bill for 1,417 Swiss francs charged to Napoleon's troops for an opulent meal and other amenities in 1797. Although a lavish feast had been prepared for Napoleon, the General merely drank a glass of water and moved on.

In 1793, a girl in Tourcoing, France, was born with only one eye—in the center of her forehead! Otherwise normal, the girl lived to the age of 15.

Canine Comparisons

Of the many thousands of dogs registered by the American Kennel Club, in 1970, there were only four breeds in which there were less than five dogs registered. It appears that throughout the entire United States, there were only four Sussex Spaniels on record, only three Belgian Malinois, only two Field Spaniels, and only two English Foxhounds.

Compare these, for example, with 61,042 Dachshunds, or with 13,180 Great Danes, or even with 769 Irish Wolfhounds.

Women as young as six and as old as 62 have become mothers, while men as young as 13 and as old as 100 have become fathers.

The fastest train in the world is the Japanese National Railroad's Hikari run, between Kyoto and Nagoya. The Hikari makes the 83-mile trip in only 47 minutes, for an average speed of 106.5 miles per hour.

A Rude Shock

In 1864, an Australian named Siegfried Marcus was experimenting with the lightbulb, and he wasn't very successful. He ignited a mixture of gasoline and air, believing he would at last be producing illumination. He was right. But he also produced a violent explosion, jolting him into the discovery that his mixture could be a method of powering a vehicle. The drawback, however, was that his contraption required a strong man to lift the rear end of the vehicle while the wheels were being spun to get the engine going. Like almost all inventors, Marcus was a bit crazy;

and after 10 years, he lost interest in the automobile, calling it "a senseless waste of time and effort."

By this time, the steam vehicle was already coming under public pressure because of the noise it engendered. Moreover, the steam engine was considered downright dangerous, and so it was common for early motorists to find the roadway blocked with barricades.

Chocolate, the bane of adolescent complexions and bulgy midriffs, is a preparation made from the seeds of the cacao tree. The Aztecs favored a chocolate beverage which they introduced to the Spanish explorers in the 16th century. This beverage found its way to Europe, where it soon became all the rage. Many chocolate shops became centers of political discussion, such as the famous *Cocoa Tree* in London.

A celebrated Chinese artist of the 1920s, Huang Erhnan, painted beautiful designs on silk cloth—with his tongue as a brush.

If in 1600, you happened to be walking along a Dutch canal, you might have been surprised to see a two-masted ship bearing down on you. Not in the canal—on the road. There was one such ship that was said to have reached a speed of 20 m.p.h. while carrying 28 fear-stricken passengers. In his notebooks, Leonardo da Vinci had envisioned some sort of self-propelled vehicle; and some Dutchman, quite naturally, had modeled such a vehicle after a sailing vessel.

Twelve architects spent most of their lives working on the construction of St. Peter's Church, in Rome. Most of them never lived to see the church completed.

The Whyos, a Brooklyn gang of mobsters who preceded the Five Points gang, issued a printed list for potential clients: "Punching, $2; both eyes blacked, $4; nose and jaw broken, $10; jacked out (stunned with a blackjack), $15; ear chewed off, $15; leg or arm broken, $19; shot in leg, $25; stabbed, $25; doing the big job, $100."

During the 21-year-plus London run of the Agatha Christie play *The Mousetrap*, wardrobe mistress Maisie Wilmer-Brown ironed her way through 36 miles of shirts.

Around 1850, a chap by the name of Loy, who lived in London, made a most unusual pair of skates. The springs across the instep and across the heel secured the skate to the foot without using screws. The skate was made of satinwood, and enriched by plates of gilded metalwork. A swan's neck was a graceful and appropriate ornament.

The Whole Story

Next to apple pie, nothing is considered more American than the doughnut. During the two World Wars, special doughnut-making machines went from one battle area to another to provide soldiers with this favorite American treat.

So it may come as quite a surprise to learn that the doughnut is not American. It was brought over from the Netherlands more than 300 years ago by the Dutch colonists, and then became a popular accompaniment to coffee and milk.

The trunk of an elephant can hold six quarts of water—enough to wash down the biggest snootful of peanuts.

Batman

During the 1930's, Clem Sohn of Lansing, Michigan, justly earned the nickname "Batman." The air-show performer fashioned a set of canvas wings and attached them to his arms, fitted a canvas web between his legs, and then jumped from airplanes at altitudes of up to 20,000 feet! Sohn looked much like the comic strip character Batman as he glided through the air in his wings and goggles, floating downward some three miles and then opening his parachute for the final descent.

Sohn soared through the air with the greatest of ease more than 2,000 times. Then, on April 25, 1937, at Vincennes, France, 100,000 horrified spectators watched as the 26-year-old daredevil's parachute failed to open and he plunged to his death.

The next time your day at the beach is ruined by cloudy skies, just remember this: without clouds and the other constituents of the earth's atmosphere, the surface of our planet would reach a temperature of 176 degrees at the equator by day, and -220 degrees at night!

Time for Tea

It is believed the first shipment of tea to the United States arrived in New Amsterdam about 1650. At the time, tea cost from $30 to $50 a pound, and in addition to making a refreshing drink, the used leaves were sometimes salted and eaten with butter.

Tea traveled with the pioneers who explored and settled our vast land. No wagon train headed West without a good supply of tea on board. Then, as now, it was the drink for people on the go who needed a lift that relaxes and refreshes.

Today, the United States is the second largest consumer of tea in the world, surpassed only by Great Britain. We are the only country that prepares large quantities of tea using three different types: loose, teabags, and instant.

The big fish fight, and fight hard, so game fishing is usually considered a man's sport. But on May 6, 1950, Mrs. H.A. Bradley took her boat out to Cape Charles, Virginia, and brought to gaff the largest drum fish ever caught—an 87-pound, 8-ounce giant!

Home, Sweet Homeless

John Howard Payne won lasting fame by writing a single song, the nostalgic *Home, Sweet Home*. Yet Payne virtually never had a home of his own!

Born in New York City in 1791, Payne spent most of his life on the move, homeless and often penniless. An actor, playwright, composer, and for a time, prison inmate, Payne died in Tunis, North Africa, where he was employed by the U.S. consulate. Today, the home in East Hampton, Long Island, where Payne spent part of his childhood, is maintained as a shrine, for the humble cottage is probably the only home, sweet home that Payne ever knew.

The Western madam known as Diamond-tooth Lil owed her nickname to a gold front tooth studded with a large diamond. Immortalized by Mae West's portrayal in a movie called *Diamond Lil*, the Austrian-born madam accumulated husbands as easily as diamonds—she married eight times without bothering with the formality of a divorce.

Babies have been known to hiccup several hours before birth. In some instances an unborn baby has cried loudly enough to be heard from 25 feet away.

The Egyptian plover has worked out a mutually satisfactory arrangement with the crocodile: the bird gets food and the crocodile gets service. The plover rides on the crocodile's back and serves as a lookout, emitting shrill cries when danger seems imminent. The plover also digs parasites out of the crocodile's back. When the crocodile finishes its dinner, the big reptile opens up its mouth so that its small helper can hop inside, and pick its teeth clean of uneaten food.

You'll need more than a set of strong glasses to read the copy of Omar Khayyam's *Rubaiyat* in the Bodelian Library at Oxford University—you'll need a microscope! This book—the smallest in the world—is only one-quarter inch high and three-sixteenths of an inch wide, and weighs just 1/327 of an ounce.

Texas has flown the flags of six nations: Spain, France, Mexico, the Republic of Texas, the United States, and the Confederate States of America.

The Republic of Texas, with its famed Lone Star flag, remained an independent nation for nearly a decade before being annexed by the United States in 1845.

The penknife with the greatest number of blades is the Year Knife, made by Joseph Rodgers & Sons, Ltd. of Sheffield, England. Built in 1822 with 1,822 blades, the knife has continued to match the year ever since. The knife will finally run out of space for further blades in the year 2,000.

A Long Talk

At 12:30 p.m. on June 12, 1935, Senator Huey Long of Louisiana began a filibuster in the Senate. When Long finally dropped into his seat from physical exhaustion at 4 a.m. the following day, he had been speaking continually for 15½ hours—the longest speech on record. The speech was 150,000 words long and included such irrelevancies as cooking recipes and humorless anecdotes. Long's marathon monologue filled 100 pages in the *Congressional Record,* and cost the Government $5,000 to print.

During the 12th century, Sutoku, Emperor of Japan, spent a three-year exile copying the *Lankauarn Sutra*—a Buddhist religious work containing 10,500 words—in his own blood.

A curlew can fly non-stop for more than 2,000 miles. Most of the bird's flight is over water, so the curlew doesn't have much of a choice about taking a breather. He can't swim!

In the 16th century, the Spaniards introduced the musket, a firearm which enabled a marksman to hit a target 400 yards away. The intricate reloading procedure of the musket necessitated the additional defense of a pike. This drawback of the musket led to the invention of the bayonet. Rifles were introduced in the 18th century; and by the 19th century, they became the standard firearm of all infantry.

Australian aborigines are not in the least ashamed of their nakedness, and don't mind defecating in view of others. But they are quite embarrassed to be seen eating. Think of the problems such mores could create in one of our crowded cities!

We are put to no end of trouble by a 10-inch snowfall—traffic is snarled, electricity fails, drains overflow, roofs leak. Imagine how the people of Tamarack, California, must have felt in the winter of 1906-7, when 884 inches of snow fell in one heap. That's 73 feet, a world's record.

Some of the plants that provide man with food can be poisonous if other parts of the plant are eaten. You may love cherries, but don't eat the cherry tree's foliage—it's toxic enough to kill. Enjoy rhubarb pie, but don't munch on the leaf blades, or it could be your last meal. The leaves of the elderberry plant are poisonous—and so are the foliage and acorns of the oak. And that rhododendron that might be flourishing in your home will spell doom for anyone who nibbles on it.

A Breach of Fashion

Until the time of the French Revolution, most men wore knee breeches rather than trousers. But in 1789, supporters of the Revolution separated themselves from the royalists by adopting trousers. Accordingly, they were know as the *sans-culottes* ("without breeches").

In token of their sympathy with the French rebels, many ordinary Americans sported trousers between 1790 and 1800. But it was not until a decade or so later that trousers substituted for breeches on formal occasions. The first President who habitually dressed in long trousers was James Madison.

Like Father, Like Son

In early 18th-century France, the office of Chief Executioner was, like many positions, handed down from father to son. So when Chief Executioner Charles Jean-Baptiste Sanson died in 1726, the job passed to his son Charles. But the young Sanson was unable to lift, much less wield, the heavy executioner's ax—he was but seven years old at the time.

The prepubescent official was forced to employ an assistant, named Prudhomme, to perform the actual decapitations, although Sanson had to be present at every execution. Finally, at age 13, the seasoned Chief Executioner was deemed strong enough to perform the dirty deed himself.

A Stroke of Luck

William Northmore, an inveterate gambler from Okehampton, England, lost his entire fortune of $850,000 on the turn of one card. The townspeople of Okehampton felt so sorry for Northmore that they elected him to Parliament in 1714, and in every election thereafter until his death.

The longest recorded drive of all time is 445 yards, achieved by E.C. Bliss in 1913. Playing on the Old Course at Herne Bay, Kent, England, Bliss—a 12-handicap player—put all of his 182 pounds behind his swing and sent the ball flying over a quarter of a mile. There was a 57-foot drop over the course of the drive. On that particular day, Bliss was blessed with luck, for a registered surveyor was on the scene to accurately measure his shot forthwith.

Chow Hound

A dog may be man's best friend, but that friendship can be pushed beyond its limits. In parts of China, roast dog is considered a gourmet's delight. The Chinese have gone so far as to develop a special breed of dog for the table, a type of chow, with black-haired dogs the most desirable.

Our slang word for food, *chow*, may or may not be linked to the edible dog of China. A Cantonese word pronounced *chow* means "fried." The word appears in the name of America's most popular Chinese dish, chow mein.

"**F**rench" ice cream is definitely different from other varieties in this country, for only ice cream made with eggs can legally be sold as "French."

The Big Shake-up

Seismologists estimate that more than 500,000 earthquakes occur each year, of which about 100,000 can be felt by people in the vicinity of the quake. But only about 1,000 quakes— or .2 percent—cause damage of any kind.

Although the instrument that measures the intensity of earthquakes, the seismograph, was not invented until almost a century later, many scientists believe that the most powerful earthquake of modern times occurred on November 1, 1755, in Lisbon, Portugal. Within six minutes of the main shock, more than 30,000 persons were dead and 12,000 dwellings were destroyed. The fire that followed the quake burned for six days.

The Lisbon quake was so powerful that cities in Morocco, hundreds of miles away, were badly damaged. And lakes in Norway were disturbed—over 2,000 miles from the center of the quake!

Although the Romans took baths and had excellent plumbing facilities for hot and cold water more than 2,000 years ago, the habit of bathing died out during the Middle Ages. Baths were usually taken only on a doctor's request. The result was a lack of hygiene that encouraged infection. Even the United States did not get its first bathtub until 1840.

Some cicadas live underground for 17 years, then emerge for a few weeks of sunshine before dying.

The Fire Extinguished by an Iceberg

The fateful voyage of the British liner *Titanic* was marred by disaster from the very beginning. As the 46,000-ton vessel left its dock in Southhampton on April 10, 1912, a fire broke out in a bunker. Four days later, when the mammoth liner struck an iceberg and went down in the North Atlantic, the fire was still burning.

A Spirited History

The use of liquor is so widespread that almost every country in the world utilizes some native product to make an alcoholic beverage. Asian liquors, distilled from rice, from millet, or from palm sap originated around 400 B.C., and took the names of *sautchoo*, *arrack*, *arika*, and *skhou*. Around the year 300, Ireland brewed up some *usquebaugh* from oat and barley beer. Around the year 900, Italy began distilling grapes to produce brandy. Around 1500, the Scots got the hand of making whiskey from malted barley. In 1750, France distilled cognac from grapes.

A play by Sinclair Lewis entitled *It Can't Happen Here* opened in 21 theatres in 18 cities—on the same night of October 27, 1936.

In case you've forgotten: the face of Woodrow Wilson adorns the U.S. Treasury's $100,000 note. And, of course, Salmon Portland Chase appears on the $10,000 bill.

The eggplant was once known as the "love apple" in England because it was thought to possess aphrodisiac properties. Botanists in northern Europe dubbed the eggplant *mala insana*, or "mad apple," because they thought that eating the fruit could result in insanity!

Specialists in brolliology—the study of the umbrella, that is—are reluctant to estimate the number of umbrellas in use throughout the world, but the country with the highest per capita use of the gamp is definitely England. As late as 1954, 300,000 umbrellas were produced in the British Isles each month! Today, most umbrellas are imported from Hong Kong and Japan. And close to 75,000 umbrellas are lost each year on the bus and underground system of London alone!

The wedding cake of the ancient Greeks was almost always a cheesecake covered with honey. The island of Samos was noted throughout Greece as the home of great cheesecake.

Gazelles, prairie dogs, wild asses, and many other animals never drink water. They have a special chemical process which transforms a part of their solid food into water.

Dubious Honor

In April of 1972, a little-known world title was lost at Beaver, Oklahoma. Governor David Hall of that state, who a year earlier had hurled a hand-sized wad of cow dung a whopping 94 feet to win the World Dung-Throwing Championship, managed a throw of only 68 feet and was dethroned by former Governor Dewey Bartlett, who broke all records with a stunning toss of 138 feet.

The invention of the first mechanical clock has been attributed to I'Hsing and Liang Ling-tsan of China, circa 725 A.D.

Tea Lore

The usual tea sold in the supermarket is a blend of 20 to 30 different varieties, each chosen for a certain characteristic—color, flavor, bouquet, body.

There are three different types of tea—black, green, and oolong. All three types come from the same tea bushes. It's how the leaves are processed after they are picked that makes the teas different.

Over 97 percent of all the tea consumed in the United States is black tea. In the processing, the tea is fully fermented.

Green tea is light in color when brewed. In its processing, it is not fermented at all.

Oolong tea is a compromise between black and green tea. It is semi-fermented, so that the leaves turn greenish brown.

The largest clams in the world weigh close to 500 pounds.

A California law makes it illegal to shoot any game bird or animal from an automobile—except a whale!

A respectable marathon runner today can cover 26 miles over a smoothly paved track in less than two-and-a-half hours, for an average speed of about ten miles per hour.

But in 1764, an English barrister named Foster Powell covered the 50 miles between London and Bath, England, in just seven hours—walking! Although almost the entire route wound over cobblestone and dirt roads, Powell walked at a rate of better than seven miles per hour.

Surprisingly, Jupiter—the largest planet in the solar system—has the shortest day of all the planets. Jupiter completes a rotation on its axis in less than ten earth hours.

The deepest lake in the world is Lake Baykal, in the Soviet Union. At some points it is more than a mile deep.

Many people believe that Charles Lindbergh was the first man to complete a transatlantic airplane flight. Actually, the feat had been accomplished many times before Lindbergh's historic flight in 1927. Eight years earlier, a crew of six U.S. Navy flyers had crossed the Atlantic in a Curtiss hydroplane, landing in the Azores before continuing on to England. Later in the same year, two Englishmen accomplished the first nonstop crossing, traveling from Newfoundland to Ireland in just over 16 hours. Their gear included two stuffed black cats. Including airship crews, Lindbergh was actually the 81st person to fly across the Atlantic Ocean. But he was the first to do it alone.

At many a fiesta held in rural Mexico, one of the treats enjoyed by the guests is ant candy. This unusual confection consists of the bodies of ants which gather honey from a species of oak leaf. The ants swell enormously until they are about the size of gooseberries. After the ants' legs and heads are removed, their bodies are piled on dishes and served as candy. The taste of these insects is very similar to that of a sweet, juicy fruit.

A corkscrew of recent invention consists of a needle attached to a pellet of carbon-dioxide. The needle pierces the cork, and a pump pushes the CO_2 into the bottle until the pressure inside the bottle ejects the cork. At least, that's the way the device is supposed to work. Frequently, the pressure will explode the bottle itself instead of the cork.

In the Book of Esther, it is stated that when the candidates for the Persian queenship were assembled by King Ahasuerus, they were brought to the royal harem and there treated for "six months with balm and six months with spices."

There are an estimated 400 to 500 different names for the cheeses produced around the world, but many of these names are merely different terms for one cheese commonly produced in an area. Actually, there are but 18 or 19 distinct varieties of cheese.

A large Hawaiian fish is called by natives an "O." A much smaller Hawaiian fish is the "homomomonukunukuaguk."

Anteojos is the Spanish word for eyeglasses. Anteojos comes from two Spanish words. *Ante* means "in front of" and *ojos* means "eyes." So *anteojos* means "in front of the eyes," which is exactly where eyeglasses belong.

Willy Ferrero, born in Rome, Italy, in 1907, made musical history only a few years after coming into the world. He conducted an orchestra in Paris when he was only four years old!

You won't find many picnic tables in the sandy plateau region of southwestern Africa, but in a pinch you could spread your lunch on top of the *Welwitschia mirabilis* plant. The trunk of this grotesque giant is often six feet in diameter, yet rises just a few inches above the ground, with an almost flat top. This bizarre form give the *Welwitschia* the appearance of a slightly folded round table!

From around the rim of this trunk extend a number of long, leathery leaves that curl like ribbons over the surrounding soil. These leaves can measure as much as 18 feet in length—long enough to be bent over and used as a table cloth!

The Ruwanweli Pagoda in Anuradhapura, Sri Lanka (Ceylon), is built on a 500-square-foot, seven-inch-thick foundation of solid silver.

Over 65 percent of the world's population goes through the day without coming in contact with a newspaper, radio, television, or telephone.

The United States is by far the world's largest importer of spices and herbs. In 1968, this country imported over 150 million pounds of spices, with a value in excess of $60 million.

Itinerant lecturer Walter Stolle had pedaled an estimated 270,000 miles in his lifetime—that's about 11 times around the earth! In his travels, Stolle has pedaled through some 140 nations, and suffered 26 robberies en route.

The Venus flytrap is actually misnamed, for the plant feeds primarily on ants and not flies. But it can digest any insect, or meat in any form. Flytraps have been known to snare creatures as large as a small frog!

A sign painted on a glass window will read differently from outside the store than it will from the inside—with the exception of the sign on the Yreka Bakery, in Yreka, California.

In October, 1937, the Russian icebreaker *Sedov* sailed from Murmansk, U.S.S.R. Arctic ice soon closed in around the ship, imprisoning it off the coast of Siberia. The ship drifted with the ice pack for 3,000 miles over Arctic seas until a new Soviet icebreaker came to its rescue, freeing a path to the open sea.

The next time the 15-man crew of the *Sedov* saw Murmansk was in January, 1940—27 months after they embarked!

We have no idea if the crew members were paid overtime.

A Timely Tale

In the famous cathedral of Notre Dame de Dijon in France, there is the oldest gong clock in the world. Given to the town of Dijon in 1383 by Philip the Hardy, this clock has been keeping abreast of the time ever since. Constructed by Jacques Marc, the clock contains two large bronze figures which have struck the hour every hour for the last 590 years. An ambitious mathematician computed that by January 1, 1950, these bronze figures had struck the clock 32,284,980 times.

For $350, a New York chocolatier will shape a bust of your head from solid chocolate.

Eureka!

In 214 B.C., a powerful Roman force attacked the city of Syracuse, the home of Archimedes, the great mathematician and astronomer. To hold off the Roman legions, the Greek inventor devised one ingenious weapon after another. Among these weapons was the catapult, which sent a ton of stones flying as far as 600 feet.

But Archimedes' most ingenious contraption was an arrangement of mirrors that directed the concentrated rays of the sun on the Roman ships and set them ablaze.

Maria Gilbert was acclaimed one of the most beautiful women in the world—not by her given name, but as dancer Lola Montez. Other renowned performers who have come to fame under pseudonyms are: John Barrymore (John Blythe); Dave Evans (Frances Octavia Smith); Gypsy Rose Lee (Rose Louise Hovick); Carole Lombard (Jane Alice Peters); Soupy Sales (Milton Hines); and Margot Fonteyn (Margaret Hookham).

On July 18, 1938, pilot Douglas "Wrongway" Corrigan took off from New York on a flight to Los Angeles, and the following day earned his nickname by touching down in Dublin, Ireland. Corrigan blamed a mistake in his compass setting for the colossal navigational error.

The nation with the highest reported murder rate is Luxembourg, with 14.4 murders per 100,000 population. The lowest reported rate is that of Norway, 0.1 per 100,000. The United States rate is 8.5.

The American bicycle industry was born in 1877, when Colonel Albert A. Pope of Boston commissioned the Weed Sewing Machine Company to make 50 "Columbia" bikes in a corner of their shop in Hartford, Connecticut. Bicycle manufacture quickly became one of America's leading mass production industries. By 1892, applications for bicycle patents had grown so numerous that the U.S. Patent Office had to establish a special department for cycles and their parts.

On October 8, 1929, a milestone in modern transportation was reached when a newsreel and two cartoons were shown on a Transcontinental Air Transport plane.

On June 13, 1948, a Los Angeles resident named Jack O'Leary caught a fit of hiccoughs. It was not until June 1,1956—about 160 million hiccoughs later—that the fit ended. During that time, the unfortunate Mr. O'Leary lost 64 pounds, and received through the mail over 60,000 suggested cures for hiccoughs.

When active, the Paricutin volcano in central Mexico could spew 4 million pounds of rock and lava into the air in one minute.

Even when you're standing still, you're actually traveling at incredibly high speeds. The earth is revolving at the speed of 1,000 miles per hour, and orbiting the sun at the speed of 66,700 miles per hour.

There are 156 languages in the world—each of which is spoken by at least one million people.

A mother cod can lay as many as five million eggs at a single spawning—of which only a half dozen usually survive. If all cod eggs produced live fish, there would be no room left in the ocean for water.

The Rinconada Racetrack in Venezuela—called the most luxurious track in the world—has a swimming pool for horses.

Pint-sized Pauline

Many people have laid claim to the title of "world's smallest adult human," but only one justly deserved that title. In 1876, Pauline Musters was born in Holland to normal-size parents. At birth, she measured 12 inches, against the normal baby's 20 to 22 inches. Throughout the rest of her life, Pauline grew only 11 inches!

When appearing in public exhibitions, Pauline was billed at 19 inches. But shortly before she died in New York City at age 19, she was measured at 23.2 inches—making her the smallest mature human on record. Her feet never measured more than four inches in length.

During the Civil War, the Union Army lost more men as a result of disease than it lost in battle. The same was true of the American armed forces serving in the Spanish-American War and World War I. In the Mexican War, the United States suffered 1,733 battle deaths—and lost 11,550 men to "other causes."

William Frederick Cody, better known as "Buffalo Bill," was well deserving of his nickname. When Cody was 21 years old, he was hired as a buffalo hunter by a firm supplying food to workers laying tracks for the Kansas Pacific Railroad. Using a 50-calibre Springfield rifle, "Buffalo Bill" earned his nickname by slaying—by his own count—4,280 buffalo in a period of 17 months.

Flavored spirits, including gin, aquavit, absinthe, and zubrovka, are produced by redistilling alcohol with a flavoring agent. Juniper is used to flavor gin; caraway seeds to flavor aquavit.

The world's largest airline is state-owned Aeroflot of the U.S.S.R., with some 1,300 craft and 400,000 employees. The largest commercial carrier in the world is United Air Lines, with about 365 craft. But surprisingly, private planes in the United States carry about 50 times as many passengers per year as all American-owned scheduled airlines combined!

Funeral directors in California are offering a new economy deal—for only $25 your ashes will be scattered over the Pacific Ocean from a light aircraft. A certificate will be issued guaranteeing the time at which your ashes were "committed to the elements of the eternal seven seas."

In 18th-century America, portraitists journeyed from town to town with an assortment of paintings of men and women, complete in every feature except the faces. A person wishing to sit for his portrait simply had to select the body he liked best, and let the artist fill in the missing face and hair.

If you're ever hightailing it from a bear in the woods, don't try the old trick of climbing a tree to escape. Almost all bears can climb trees.

As late as the sixteenth century, many oculists remained skeptical of eyeglasses. In 1583, Dr. Georg Bartisch of Dresden, one of the most famous oculists of his time, advised patients to do without spectacles. "A person sees and recognizes something better when he has nothing in front of his eyes than when he has something there," the doctor reasoned. "It is much better that one should preserve his two eyes than that he should have four."

Since their formation 10,000 years ago, the Niagara Falls have eaten their way seven miles upstream. If they continue at that rate, they will disappear into Lake Erie in 22,800 years.

The spoon as we know it today, with its spatulate handle, dates from only the 18th century.

Glass, though it feels hard enough to be called a solid, is actually a liquid. If left standing in one position, the particles that make up glass will flow downward.

Since the 19th century, the *Tour d'Argent*—the oldest restaurant in Paris—has given a memento ticket to every diner who orders the specialty of the house, *canard rouennais*. The name and number of the guest is entered in a visitors' book, a unique record which has now reached six figures. Ticket number 112,151 went to President Franklin D. Roosevelt; 203,728 to Marlene Dietrich; and 253,652 to Charlie Chaplin.

Only eight breeds of purebred dog originated in the United States: the American foxhound, American water spaniel, Boston terrier, Chesapeake Bay retriever, Coonhound, Amertoy, Spitz, and Staffordshire terrier. The British Isles holds the pedigreed pooch title—of the world's 163 recognized breeds, 47 originated there.

The first successful electric elevator was installed in the Demarest Building in New York City, in 1889.

A Shaggy Dog Story

Between 1892 and 1902, a small mongrel named Tim—with a metal collection box attached to his collar—met all incoming trains in London's Paddington Station to beg for coins for the widows' and orphans' fund of a British railroad. When the animal died, his body was placed in a glass case in the station, with a slot for coins so that the dog could continue his work.

Airborne Thievery

The tropical man-of-war, or frigate bird, likes a fish dinner. But it doesn't fish in the way most birds do. Instead, it waits until another bird has done the work. Then it swoops down and beats the bird with its wings. The unlucky bird, trying to defend itself, lets go of the fish. The swift man-of-war dives, snatches the fish, and zooms away.

Sometimes this robber does its own fishing in mid-air above the ocean. It dives down and grabs flying fish when they sail above water.

The term *pekoe* refers only to a size of tea leaf—and not to a type or variety of tea. Other names of sizes are *Orange Pekoe, Souchong, Broken Pekor, Fannings,* and *Dust*.

Beards were once placed under government control in Romania. Whiskers could be worn only if the owner secured an official permit, and paid the appropriate fee.

Don't ever accuse the chicken of being behind the times. In the 1930s, the average American hen laid 121 eggs a year. Today, a hen donates about 217 eggs to the breakfast tables of America.

Bet you think that Big Ben is a clock in London. This is a popular misapprehension, even in England. Actually, Big Ben is the name of the hour bell in the *Westminster* clock!

The Moscow to Peking run on the Trans-Siberian Railroad is the longest rail journey that can be made without changing trains.

Vodka is an unaged spirit obtained from potatoes or grain. It is then filtered through vegetable charcoal. In the United States, this process produces a liquid that must be "without distinctive character, aroma, or taste," but which packs quite a noticeable wallop at over 190 proof.

Divorce, Moslem style: According to the laws of Islam, a Moslem husband can divorce any of his four lawful wives by simply saying "I divorce you" three times. Wives do not have the same privilege.

The female cuckoo of Europe searches out the egg-filled nest of some hard-working bird and lays her single egg in that nest. Then the cuckoo picks up one of the eggs of its host, drops that egg on the ground, and flies away, never to return, hoping that the substitution won't be noticed. If the returning mother recognizes the strange egg as an interloper, she jabs a hole in it, and rolls it out of the nest.

The day was August 19, 1962. Longview, Texas was agog. Homero Blancas, a 24-year-old graduate of the University of Houston, had just completed the first round of the Premier Invitational Tournament in 55 strokes! His card of 27 for the front nine and 28 for the back was the lowest round of golf ever played on a course measuring more than 5,000 yards.

One of the most spectacular homing-pigeon flights of all time took place in 1931, when a bird that had been taken from its home in Saigon was released in Arras, France, and found its way over completely unfamiliar territory to its Far-Eastern home. The bird made the trip in just 24 days.

The nation with the highest beer consumption is Belgium. The average Belgian enjoys 30.6 gallons of the frothy nectar each year. In the Northern Territory of Australia, however, beer consumption has been unofficially estimated to be close to 52 gallons per person each year.

The longest of all worms is the *Lineus longissimus*, or "living fishing line worm." In 1964, a specimen washed ashore at St. Andrews, Scotland, after a storm. It measured more than 180 feet in length.

The longest bicycle ever constructed was a tandem bike that could seat 10. The machine was 23 feet long and weighed 305 pounds.

A spider's web is so lightweight that if one ounce of the material were stretched into a thin strand, it could reach across the Atlantic Ocean.

Pitcher Cy Young holds all of the following baseball pitching records: most wins, most complete games, most innings pitched; he ranks fourth in total shutouts, and fourth in strikeouts. One statistic in which Young does not rank among the leaders is bases on balls.

The all-time most generous pitcher in baseball history is Early Wynn, who dished out 1,775 walks during his career.

Ostriches feed unhatched eggs to their young. Several female ostriches often lay their eggs in a single nest during the mating season. They add a few each day until there is a total of two dozen. Some of these eggs hatch earlier than others. To feed their hungry babies who cannot eat the rough food of the adult ostrich, the parent birds crack open the unhatched eggs and feed them to their youngsters.

Polly Want a Cracker!

The size of a parrot's vocabulary depends upon a variety of factors: the patience and perseverance of the trainer; the age at which the parrot is trained; and of course, the talent of the individual bird. Well-trained birds can accumulate a vocabulary of a few hundred words, but several birds have been taught to utter fairly complex sentences or passages.

There have been fairly reliable reports that a certain parrot was trained to recite the Lord's Prayer entire. According to the United States Biological Survey, there is no reason to doubt the claim on biological grounds.

The Facts on Fossils

A fossil can be either the actual remains of a plant or an animal, or the imprint of a plant or animal, preserved from prehistoric times by nature. Quick burial in material that excludes bacteria and oxygen prevents decay and permits whole preservation. Preservation for aeons creates fossils. The scientific study of fossils is called paleontology.

Insects that lived millions of years ago are often found in amber. This hard substance was originally a sticky resin which enveloped the insect. Through the years, the fragile tissues of the insect dried, until all that remained was the mold, sometimes so precise scientists can conduct microscopic studies of its structure.

Fossilization is often the result of petrification. Mineral material from underground streams may be deposited in the interstices of bones, shells, or plants, and render the subject more stonelike, thus protecting it from the ravages of time. Over the millennia, the original live material may be replaced entirely by minerals, so that the original structure and appearance are maintained, as in petrified wood. Petrified logs from the Triassic period may be seen in the Petrified Forest of Arizona.

Jeweled Jahangir

Of the many collectors of glittering jewels down through the ages, Emperor Jahangir, the noble ruler of India who died in 1627, is the most noted who ever lived. It is reported that he owned a total of 2,235,600 carats of pearls, 931,500 carats of emeralds, 376,600 carats of rubies, 279,450 carats of diamonds, and 186,300 carats of jade.

For his time, Jahangir was an enlightened monarch. During his reign, architectural masterpieces rose throughout India.

One of the emperor's hobbies was fishing, but Jahangir never killed a fish he caught. Instead, he would place a string of pearls through the fish's gills and throw it back into the water.

If nothing else, the man was extremely vain, for his name itself, Jahangir, means "Conqueror of the World." In addition, he had other glorious titles such as "Possessor of the Planets," "Mirror of the Glories of God," and "King of Increasing Fortune."

Assuming that the earth were completely dry, a man walking day and night at a steady pace could circumnavigate the planet in a little less than a year. A tidal wave could accomplish a round trip in just 60 hours; a bullet, in 14 hours; and a beam of light in just one-tenth of a second.

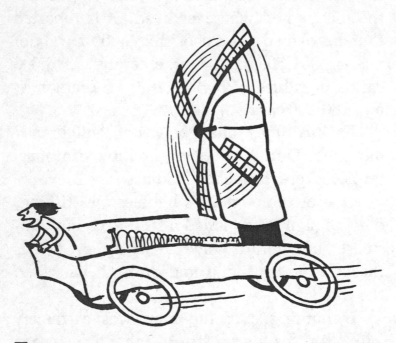

About 1700, a Swiss inventor mounted a windmill on a wagon. It was hoped that as the windmill wound up a huge spring, the vehicle would lope along under its own power.

An Enlightening Account

Man is not a nocturnal creature; his eyes do not adjust to darkness as well as do those of an owl. When early man discovered the secret of fire, he soon thereafter discovered how to brighten his night with a torch or a candle.

The candle probably evolved when a piece of wood, or rush, or cord fell into ignited fat. How astounding it must have been to realize that the foreign body was not immediately consumed.

In the late 18th and early 19th centuries, candles were made of tallow, beeswax, and vegetable wax, such as bayberry. During the past decade, there has been a great revival in candlemaking, especially of the organically scented varieties.

The first lamp was probably a dish which contained oil and a wick. The next development, thought to have originated in Egypt, was the float-wick lamp; here the wick was supported *above* the oil.

One inch of rain contains the same amount of water as a ten-inch snowstorm.

Hebrew had been a dead language for 2,300 years before it was revived by the Jews in Israel as their common language. There is no other case in which a dead language has been resurrected.

An age-old myth held that certain precious gems could produce offspring. Pearl divers in Borneo often placed a pair of pearls together in the hope that the two gems would mate and have a family.

A Surfeit of Smiths

Most Americans are aware that Smith is the most common surname in this country— nearly one in every 100 Americans is named Smith. And with John the most common first name here, there are indeed a great number of John Smiths in the United States. Think of the problem this superabundance of John Smiths causes for official record keepers. The U.S. Veterans Administration alone has had 13,000 John Smiths on its roles at the same time—8,000 with no middle name or initial!

An Arboreal Affair

Among the Brahmans of southern India, a younger brother may not marry before an older one. When there is no bride available for the senior brother, he is often married to a tree, which leaves the younger brother free to take a wife. Sometimes the tree marriage takes place at the same time as the regular marriage, in the belief that some evil influence which would otherwise attach to the newly wedded pair will be diverted to the tree.

The first boardwalk erected in the United States was located in Atlantic City, New Jersey. The eight-foot wide walkway was completed in 1870 and rested directly on top of the sand.

In 1970, a limbo dancer from the West Indies, Theresa Marquis, limboed her way under a bar only six and one half inches above the ground. Try to match that record.

A Nose for Music

You may have an ear for music, but to master one peculiar native instrument, you'll need a nose for music as well.

The nose-flute is the favorite musical instrument of the Tinguian tribe, who live in the north of Luzon, one of the Philippine Islands. A tribesman plays the flute by blocking up one nostril and expelling air gently through the other. As the flutist breathes into the flute, he moves his fingers over holes in the instrument to produce a tune.

Not everyone believes that baseball is strictly an American tradition. In 1962, the Russian newspaper *Izvestia* claimed that "Beizbol" was an old Russian game!

For the largest amount of cold cash ever laid out for a piece of diamond jewelry, we must turn to the 69-carat ring bought at a 1969 auction by actor Richard Burton, and presented to his wife, Elizabeth Taylor. The gem set Burton back a neat $1.2 million!

The fastest dog in the world is either the saluki or the greyhound, depending on whom you talk to. The greyhound has been clocked at 41.7 miles per hour.

The suit of armor worn by the later medieval knight offered the warrior such complete protection that many battles were fought and won without the loss of a single man. In 1423, when the Milanese defeated the Florentines at Zagonara, only three men died in the fray—and all were killed by drowning in the mud after falling from their horses.

The first published reference to stamp collecting appeared in 1841, when a woman placed an ad in an English newspaper for cancelled postage stamps she planned to use to wallpaper her dressing room. The mania for stamp collecting spread so quickly in England that by 1842, the magazine *Punch* could declare that stamp collectors "betray more anxiety to treasure the Queens' heads than Henry the Eighth did to get rid of them!"

The first bona-fide railroad in this country was the Baltimore & Ohio, which began hauling passengers and freight in 1830. The nation was first crossed with a coast-to-coast line on May 10, 1869.

The ubiquitous beer can made its first appearance in this country in 1935. There are now literally hundreds of different brands of American beer, including the likes of Dutch Treat, Cook's Goldblume, Premium Grain Belt, Fyfe & Drum, Hop'n Gator, Luck, and Short Snorter.

An otter is quick enough to dodge a rifle bullet.

The oldest alcoholic beverage we know of is mead, a wine made from honey. The sweet drink is stored in wooden casks, and must be left to mature for up to five years.

Mead is the national drink of Poland. The stiff attitude the Poles displayed while enjoying their mead prompted Napoleon to tell his troops to "drink, but in the Polish fashion."

In the middle of the 14th century, in Spain, there arose a vogue of wearing false beards. In the morning, a grandee dandy would drape his chin in a crimson beard; in the evening, he serenaded his senorita in an adjustable, long, black hanging. Soon the country resembled a huge masquerade party. No one knew who was who. Creditors could not catch up with debtors. The police arrested the innocent while villains hid behind hair. Wives were conjugal with the wrong husbands, whereupon the price of horsehair skyrocketed. King Peter of Aragon had to end the farce by forbidding the wearing of false beards.

John Paul Jones, the greatest American naval hero of the Revolutionary War, ended his military career as an admiral in the Russian navy.

In 1788, the Russian Empress Catherine the Great invited Jones to join her Imperial Navy as a rear admiral. Jones accepted the commission, and helped to lead a Russian fleet in a successful campaign against the Turks in the Black Sea.

After his death in 1792, the American hero lay buried in an unmarked grave in France for more than a century. He now lies buried at the U.S. Naval Academy in Annapolis, Maryland.

A single sheet of paper produced in 1830 by the Whitehall Mills in Derbyshire, England, measured four feet in width and *three miles* in length!

When the headmaster of a high school in Oregon began broadcasting the names of absent students every morning on the radio, truancy at his school dropped by 25 percent.

Tornadoes have been reported in every state in the continental United States, with the sole exception of Rhode Island. Iowa has reported the greatest number, averaging 15 tornadoes per 50 square miles each year. Texas has suffered the greatest property damage, and Arkansas the most fatalities.

The worst tornado in United States history struck Missouri, Indiana, and Illinois in March, 1925, killing 689 and damaging or destroying an estimated $17 million in property. In 1953, a tornado that hit, oddly enough, Massachusetts took a toll of $52 million in damages and killed 92 people, more than all the tornadoes that struck Iowa in the previous 37 years!

Talk about your fat cats! The heaviest domestic cat was a feline named Tiger, of Essex, England, who weighed 42 pounds.

From the 11,200-foot peak of Mount Izaru in Costa Rica, you can see both the Atlantic and Pacific Oceans. This is the only point in the Americas from which such a view is possible.

The crawling fish of Asia can live for a week out of water. In fact, this fish will instinctively leave a stream that is going dry and head for the nearest water, often traversing a mile or more of dry land.

The Bigger They Come, the Harder They Fall

Although only one foot long, a sea creature known as the urchin fish is capable of killing a 20-foot shark. The urchin fish is often attacked and swallowed by a shark. But once in the belly of the larger fish, the urchin fish blows up its prickly body like an inflated balloon, finally ripping apart the shark's belly and swimming out of the monster's body.

You've often wondered who holds the record for tobacco-juice spitting, right? Well, that noble distinction belongs to one Don Snyder, of Eupora, Mississippi, who in 1975, at the annual classic, spit a wad of tobacco a whopping 31 feet 1 inch.

Nicholas Joseph Cugnot of France is credited with the invention of the first automobile. Cugnot built himself a steam-powered tricycle in 1769, which attained a speed of 2 m.p.h. while carrying four people.

The largest cigar ever made—now on display in the Bunde Tobacco and Cigar Museum in Germany—is 170 centimeters (about 67 inches) long and 67 centimeters in circumference. The giant cigar would take about 600 hours to smoke.

Flight of Fancy

The world record for altitude by a model aircraft is 26,929 feet by Maynard L. Hill, of the United States, on September 6, 1970, using a radio-controlled model. The speed record is 213.71 m.p.h. by V. Goukoune and V. Myakinin with a motor piston radio-controlled model at Klementyeva, U.S.S.R. on September 21, 1971.

Seventeen harvest mice have a combined weight close to that of a 150-pound man. The mice, however, need about 17 times as much food a day as does the man.

The movie *Sleep* by Andy Warhol, the longest non-talking film ever made, consists solely of a man sleeping for eight hours.

The Australian walking fish occasionally leaves the water and climbs a tree to enjoy a snack of insects.

You can credit the French monarch Louis XVI for the uniform shape of today's handkerchiefs. At one time, hankies could be bought in almost any size and shape—round, square, oval, or whatever. According to one tale, Queen Marie Antoinette told the king she was tired of seeing handkerchiefs in all kinds of extravagant shapes. The king quickly decreed that "the length of the handkerchief shall equal the width throughout the kingdom." Since French fine-hanky makers dominated the industry for centuries, Louis' dictum became unwritten law throughout Europe.

The Crossing of the Bar

For those who cannot swim the English Channel, there are more ingenious modes of crossing that body of water, and attracting the attendant publicity. For example, one man rowed across the Channel in a coffin, while another man walked across it shod in wooden boots in the shape of flatboats. Still another enterprising individual traversed the Channel in an inflated rubber suit sporting a sail the size of a bath towel.

The Weight of Responsibility

On May 20 of each year, a ceremony known as the Weighing of the Mayor takes place in High Wycombe, England. Outside the town hall, the mayor, his wife, and a number of minor officials are each placed on the scales and their weights are announced to the assembled populace, along with the weights of the previous year's incumbents.

Dogs have been known to have litters as large as 23.

Southpaws, Take Heart

Many theories have been advanced to explain the dominance of right-handedness. One of these theories holds that the origin of this phenomenon is physiological, the result of an unequal distribution of the viscera in the abdominal cavity. A more commonly accepted view, however, is that right-handedness is primarily a product of primitive warfare. Early man was engaged in a continual struggle for survival with his fellow man. When called upon to protect himself and his family, he would instinctively protect the vital region around his heart by fending off blows with his left arm, while using his right to strike blows against his adversary. Through a long process of natural selection, those men who had powerful right arms survived to pass their hereditary characteristics on. The natural southpaws who were forced to battle with their right arms fell by the wayside.

English contains more words than any other language—800,000—but it is doubtful that any individual uses more than 60,000.

My Kingdom for a Book

João de Barros, a 16th-century Portuguese writer, once received an entire province for writing a book. As a young man of 20, Barros composed a chivalric romance entitled *Cronica do Clarimundo*, and dedicated it to Prince John of Portugal. When the Prince later became King John III, he gave the writer the vast province of Maranhão as a reward for his work.

Maranhão, in the Portuguese South American colony of Brazil, then comprised some 177,000 square miles—five times the area of Portugal itself!

The Himalaya-Karakoram Range, which stretches across the borders of China, India, and Nepal, contains almost all of the world's 60 highest mountain peaks.

Most people know that Mount Everest, the most famous Himalayan peak, is the world's tallest mountain. Do you know the name of the world's second highest peak? It's Godwin-Austen, at 28,250 feet, which lies in the Kashmir district of India.

A Shocking Tale

When attacking another fish, an electric eel can produce a current of 550 volts—more than four times the current produced by one electric wall outlet. The eel's current is produced by some 8,000 minute storage cells situated along the whole length of its body. The current runs between the eel's head, which is positive in charge, and its tail, which is negative.

Because the eel's vital nervous and swimming organs are electrically insulated by fatty tissue, an eel cannot electrocute another of its species.

The record for the most consecutive sit-ups is held by Richard John Knecht, who on December 23, 1972, did 25,222 in 11 hours, 14 minutes. He was eight years old.

The first railroad station in the United States was the Baltimore & Ohio Railroad depot in Baltimore, Maryland. The two-story building, erected in 1830, still stands.

The two favorite plays among amateur dramatic groups in the United States are currently *Ah, Wilderness!* by Eugene O'Neill, and *Barefoot in the Park* by Neil Simon.

In the early days of photography, the long exposure time necessary for an adequate shot required the photographer to attach a head clamp to the person sitting for a portrait to prevent movement and a blurred image. The clamp did much to produce the rigid, artificial facial expressions typical of most early photo portraiture.

Despite its nickname, the "Windy City" of Chicago is far from the windiest city in America. That dubious honor belongs to Great Falls, Montana, where the average wind speed is just over 13 miles per hour. Chicago does not even rank in the top ten of windy cities. Boston, Cleveland, Dallas, and Milwaukee must all contend with an average wind speed greater than that of the "Windy City."

One-Wheel Antics

In 1934, a vaudeville performer named Walter Nilsson pedaled across the United States on an 8½-foot-high unicycle—and never once fell from the bike. Nilsson completed the 3,306-mile trek in just 117 days.

The tallest unicycle was ridden by Carlho Sein Abrahams in Paramaribo, Surinam. It was 45 feet, 10 inches high.

According to legend, Henry I of England established the yard as the distance from the point of his nose to the end of his thumb when his arm was outstretched.

The Whiskerino Club

In 1922, when the city of Sacramento wanted to arrange a celebration commemorating the swashbuckling era of the forty-niners, they passed an ordinance compelling "all male citizens over the age of consent to grow whiskers and thus make the town look like it used to." Loyalty to their fair and sentimental city outweighed gallantry toward their wives and sweethearts; and all the males became so enthusiastic over the idea, they even formed a Whiskerino Club, offering a prize for the longest pair of whiskers. A natty gent, sporting passementerie some 17 feet in length, won the first prize. In keeping with the whole idea, and feeling quite hellish, the Sacramento Club also awarded a prize for "the most impressive cootie garage." There are no further statistics.

The gateway to the fortress of Purandhar, near Poona, India, is built on a foundation of solid gold. The 50,000 gold bricks in the foundation would be worth over $40 million at today's prices.

Among the unusual names for money throughout the world are: *Rupee* (India); *Cruzeiro* (Brazil); *Kyat* (Burma); *Balboa* (Panama); *Quetzal* (Guatemala); *Bolivar* (Venezuela); *Sucre* (Ecuador); *Gourde* (Haiti); and *Zloty* (Poland).

Chocolate for eating was not perfected until 1876. M.D. Peter of Switzerland turned the trick. Today, Swiss milk chocolate is universally renowned for its flavor, color, and texture. But the most popular eating chocolate in the world is the plain old Hershey Bar, produced in Hershey, Pennsylvania, in the world's largest chocolate factory. The Hershey factory turns out well over 200 million candy bars a year.

Elderly people are less likely to die in the months preceding their birthdays than in the months that follow. The death rate among the elderly is lowest in the two months before the month of birth, and peaks in the month following the birthday.

Life with Father still reigns as the all-time longest-running dramatic production in Broadway history. A number of musicals have surpassed *Life with Father*, but no non-musicals. *Tobacco Road* is second among non-musicals, with 3,182 performances, just 42 less than *Life with Father*.

Dotage

George Bernard Shaw wrote a play at the age of 93. Goethe completed his masterpiece, *Faust*, at the age of 81. W. Somerset Maugham, Leo Tolstoy, and Michelangelo all were working at age 80.

Joan of Arc was only 17 years old when she led the French army to victory against the English at Orleans. But Joan actually was not French! Her birthplace, the village of Domremy, lay within an independent duchy allied with the duchy of Lorraine. Lorraine warred frequently with France until it became part of the French kingdom in 1776.

Small "toy" dogs became popular in the British Isles when laws were enacted to control poaching pooches. The 11th-century King Canute, for one, decreed that all dogs kept within 10 miles of the king's forest preserve must have their knee joints cut to hinder them from chasing his game. But exceptions were made for any dog that could fit through a "dog gauge," a ring seven inches wide and five inches high.

The largest commercial elevator on record was constructed to raise and lower a full swimming pool on the stage of the Hippodrome Theater in New York. The device had a capacity of 250,000 pounds—that's equal in weight to 35 hippopotami—and moved at a speed of 12 feet per minute, slower than the most sluggish hippo!

It is illegal in Arizona to kick a mule—and quite foolhardy as well. A mule is not liable to prosecution for a like offense.

In Baltimore, it is a crime to mistreat an oyster.

Soda water was invented by a Philadelphia resident, Townsend Speakman, in 1807. He later added fruit juices to make the water more palatable.

Disneyland in Japan? Don't be surprised if Mickey Mouse and friends turn up in the Land of the Rising Sun by the middle of the 1980s. Present plans call for a 204-acre Disneyland amusement park near Tokyo.

Faster Than a Speeding Bullet

A movie camera has been developed for taking pictures of objects traveling at extremely high speeds. If the camera—which takes 11,000,000 pictures a second—photographed a bullet traveling at the speed of 1,900 miles per hour, three minutes of normal-speed projection would be required to show just one foot of the bullet's travel.

An English jury list surviving from 1658, which was compiled in a Puritan district, includes the baptismal names Be-thankful, Live-in-peace, Goodgift, Joy-from-above, Faint-not, More-fruit, Accepted, Stand-fast-on-high, Called, Return, Search-the-Scriptures, and Weep-not, as well as the names Earth Adams, Meek Brewer, Be-courteous Cole, and Kill-sin Pimple.

Top Dog

The greatest racing dog in history was Mick the Miller, a greyhound owned by an Irish priest named Father Brophy. Mick flashed sensational speed on the English tracks, and the Father was offered $4,000 for the beast. He accepted on condition that he receive the Derby purse if the dog won the classic. The Miller came through, winning $50,000.

In his three-year career on English soil, Mick never lost a race.

The North Magnetic Pole is commonly located at latitude 71 degrees North, longitude 96 degrees West, in the vicinity of the Boothia Peninsula on the northernmost shore of mainland North America. The South Magnetic Pole, at latitude 73 degrees South, longitude 156 degrees East, is located on the continent of Antarctica. But the exact location of the poles shifts from time to time. And the true magnetic poles are located hundreds of miles away from the "apparent" or compass-indicated poles!

You know those white blobs you see when you close your eyes? These are phosphenes— visual images produced when the retina is stimulated by pressure exerted on the eyeball through closed eyelids.

The pillory, that curiosity of Colonial America used to punish lawbreakers, was not the harmless humiliation most people presume. The pillory victim frequently incurred serious injury, even death, from severe beating inflicted by the citizenry.

Since meat preservation was a problem before the invention of refrigeration, preserved meat was always popular. In the Middle Ages, sausage makers developed individual formulas for seasoning their products, which frequently took the name of the city where they originated. Genoa salami hails, of course, from Genoa. From Frankfurt came the frankfurter; from Bologna—well, need we say more?

Most tennis historians trace the origin of the sport to a 12th and 13th-century French game called *jeu de paume*, "palm game." As you might guess, the sport was played with the palm of the hand, not a racket. The indoor court that came to be used for the game suggests a religious cloister, and the earliest references to the game are usually to be found in ecclesiastical writing, confirming that tennis probably owes its origin to French priests playing handball in a cathedral cloister.

By the way, French king Louis X reportedly died from a chill he received after a heated game of *jeu de paume* at the Vincennes courts.

Dope on Diamonds

The largest diamond ever found was the 1½-pound Cullinan diamond, unearthed in South Africa in 1905. Other notable diamonds: the Koh-i-noor, now among the British crown jewels; the Hope diamond, the largest known blue in existence; the Star of Africa No. 1, cut from the Cullinan; the Tiffany, an orange-yellow diamond; and the Dresden, a greenish diamond.

The green variety of beryl is known as emerald; the blue is aquamarine. Highly prized in antiquity, the emerald was a particular favorite in pre-Columbian Mexico and Peru. An 11,000-carat emerald was reportedly found in South Africa in 1956.

Sapphire is a variety of transparent blue corundum. It is mined primarily in Asia and Australia, though some sapphires are to be found in Montana. The "Black Star Sapphire of Queensland" is the largest cut gem-quality sapphire.

You shiver when you're cold because shivering increases muscular action and thus raises body temperature.

A honeybee can carry a burden 300 times its own weight. To equal this feat a 250-pound man would have to carry a 35-ton truck on his back.

Although mechanical refrigeration techniques have been developed only within the last 100 years, ice cream was enjoyed in Italy as early as the sixteenth century—and perhaps even earlier in England. Italian ice cream arrived in France in 1533, along with Catherine de Medici and her retinue of chefs, when the 14-year-old Florentine moved to Paris to marry King Henry II. For many years, the chefs of various French noblemen tried to keep their recipes for ice cream a secret from other chefs—and from their masters, who were frequently astounded by their cooks' talent for serving a cold dessert even in the warmest months.

Roses have been cultivated for so long that it's impossible to determine where or when the flower was first domesticated. No species of purely wild rose remain on earth.

Solace for Southpaws

There are no records of the exact beginning of discrimination against lefthanders, but as far back as Rome, right was right; which means to say that *dexter* from which comes our word *dextrous* or *handy*, means right in Latin. But how did the Romans designate the other side? Anything that was left was *sinistra* (sinister). Even the Old English, who gave us the word *left*, used it to mean *weak*. Now is that fair?

Fighting a ratio of five righthanders for every lefthander, lefthanders have risen to the challenge. Da Vinci worked with his left hand. A study of Einstein's brainwaves indicated that his right hemisphere—the side responsible for the responses on the left side of the body—was more highly developed than his left.

Today, the words "housewife" and "hussy" are almost mutually exclusive. But around 1800, the word "housewife" carried such derogatory connotations that it spawned the shorter "hussy," with its present meaning.

You may soon be able to discard the magazine rack in your bathroom. A company in West Germany now manufactures rolls of toilet paper with English lessons printed on the paper.

The longest fight in the history of boxing took place in New Orleans on April 6-7, 1893. Andy Bowen and Jack Burke fought for 110 rounds—seven hours and 19 minutes—only to have the referee break up the fight and declare it "no contest."

Cubic zirconia gems, man-made byproducts of laser technology, can reportedly pass as diamonds to almost any eye—and cost but $12 a carat!

Starfish on the Rampage

The Great Barrier Reef, the largest animal-made structure on earth, may be shrinking. Vast areas of the 1,200-mile-long reef, which was formed by tiny animals called corals, have been damaged—not by oil spills or any other man-made peril, but by a plague of crown of thorns starfish!

The starfish were first reported in large numbers during the 1960s. Since then, they have eaten their way down to the southern end of the reef, which lies off the eastern coast of Australia. Portions of the reef already ravaged by the starfish have begun to grow back, but Australian scientists fear that the hungry echinoderms may start eating their way northward again, devouring the regenerated portions of the reef.

The crown of thorns starfish derive their name from prominent, poisonous spines that cover the upper portion of their body. The starfish, which sport 16 or 17 arms and grow up to 20 inches in diameter, have been found in concentrations of up to 300,000 per square mile.

Some scientists believe the starfish plague may be the result of the activities of shell collectors and spear fishermen, who kill off many of the starfish's normal predators.

Earthquakes have probably killed more than 13 million people over the last 4,000 years. The most deadly quake of all time occurred in 1556, in Shensi Province, China, when some 830,000 people lost their lives!

The worst quake of this century occurred on September 1, 1925, destroying much of the cities of Tokyo and Yokohama, Japan. The quake—which lasted 30 seconds—and the fires that followed claimed about 143,000 lives, injured 125,000 people, and damaged property valued at an estimated $2.8 billion! The quake caused the sea bottom in a nearby bay to sink close to 1,000 feet—and tossed potatoes right out of the ground!

In 1973, a 54-year-old man in Hanover, West Germany, began hiccoughing. Two years and some 36 million hiccoughs later, the distraught German decided to end the hiccoughing bout once and for all, and leapt to his death from a hospital window.

As Old As the Hills

Perhaps the oldest living thing on Earth is the Macrozamia tree, which grows in the Tambourine Mountains of Queensland, Australia. Scientists estimate that these trees are anywhere from 12,000 to 15,000 years old—more than six times as old as the giant redwoods of California and Oregon.

Although there is some controversy over the exact age of these palmlike trees—counting their concentric rings is a very difficult task—everyone agrees that the Macrozamia is unequaled in age. The giant bald cypress of Mexico is definitely known to be 4,000 years old, and is far younger than many of the Australian Macrozamias. These trees were old when David and Goliath were boys.

Hail rarely falls in the winter. Surprisingly, the ice balls will not fall when the ground temperature is below freezing. And hail almost never forms unless a thunderstorm is occuring. Since the conditions which produce thunderstorms rarely occur in winter, hail is generally a summer phenomenon.

King Louis XIV of France owned an estimated 413 beds in his various palaces. A ribald painting called "The Triumph of Venus" originally adorned the king's favorite bed at Versailles, but his second wife, a woman of a more religious bent, had it replaced with "The Sacrifice of Abraham."

A dentifrice currently made in France tints the gums pink to make the teeth look whiter by comparison.

The squirting lapel flower is an old practical joke, but there are many specimens of the plant kingdom that do indeed squirt liquid. Among these is the aptly named squirting cucumber. When the fruit of this Mediterranean plant is ripe, the inner tissue forms a liquid in which the seeds float. The "cucumber" swells with liquid to the bursting point, then explodes and propels the juice and seed mixture through a small hole punched in the end of the fruit. The explosion is powerful enough to propel the seeds as far as 40 feet from the plant!

If ever a man tried to get to Heaven it was Ignatious Trebitsch of Hungary. Born a Jew in 1789, Trebitsch went to Germany at the age of 18, and was baptized in the Lutheran faith. Later, he removed to England, where he became a Quaker and a member of Parliament, then an Anglican curate, a German spy, and a Presbyterian missionary to Canada. After returning to Germany for awhile following World War I, Trebitsch spent the last 17 years of his life as a Buddhist monk, and died in a Shanghai monastery in 1943. Considering how much time he spent as a man of the cloth—albeit his coat was of many colors—it is hoped that Trebitsch was forgiven by God for his brief stint as a forger and convict durng his sojourn in England.

The producers of the 1947 spectacular *Caesar and Cleopatra* were perfectionists indeed. For a moonlight scene beside the Sphinx, a set was designed which showed hundreds of stars in the sky in the exact position they occupied over the Egyptian desert in the year 45 B.C.

Compared to modern footwear, the shoes of earlier centuries were, for the most part, highly uncomfortable. It wasn't until the invention in 1818 of the left-shoe last and the right-shoe last that the left shoe was constructed differently from the right shoe. Prior to that, either shoe could be worn on either foot with equal discomfort!

Mission Impossible

Evangelist John Alexander Dowie, who at the turn of the century succeeded in establishing a new religion and buying and constructing Zion City, Illinois as the official dwelling place of his converts, set out, in 1903, "to save sinful New York." Dowie, who called himself "Elijah the Restorer," brought 3,000 of his followers along to Madison Square Garden, where in the midst of the evangelist's first sermon, the entire audience walked out in disgust. After a month of failing to convert New Yorkers to Zionism—either by small daily meetings or the distribution of Zionist literature—Elijah and his "angels" departed, having spend $300,000 on their vain effort to convert New Yorkers from vanity.

A car runs more smoothly at night or in damp weather simply because the air is cooler, not because it contains more oxygen; the amount of oxygen in the air is a constant. Cool air is more dense than warm air; and therefore, an engine takes in a greater weight of air when it is damp and chilly. This accounts for the increased power and the freedom from engine knock which so many motorists notice when they drive at night or in the rain.

The total cost of constructing the Eiffel Tower in Paris was recovered from sightseers' fees during the first year after the Tower's completion.

Honolulu, Hawaii, is the American city with the highest median family income—$12,539 in 1970. The city's nearest competitors were: San Jose, California; Seattle, Washington; and Indianapolis, Indiana. At the other end of the scale were New Orleans and Miami, where median family incomes were below $7,500.

A Spicy Story

Columbus made his journey to America seeking a short way to India in order to import spices. The spices were extremely important to Europe at a time when refrigeration was not known.

Nowadays, international trade in spices amounts to something over $170 million a year. Pepper alone normally accounts for over one-fourth of the world's total trade in spices.

The Golden Touch

You've heard the phrase, "rich as Croesus"— ever wonder how rich the last king of Lydia actually was? We don't know exactly how much Croesus, who reigned from 560 B.C. to 546 B.C., was worth in dollars and cents, but the remains of an elaborate gold-refining works, uncovered by archaeologists digging at Sardis, suggest that Croesus minted his own pure gold coins. Before Croesus' time, coins were made of electrum, an alloy containing 20-35 percent silver, so Croesus' discovery of a purification process made possible the first standardization of currency.

Rainbows may be seen at night. Lunar rainbows were observed and recorded in ancient times and are not uncommon. When the sun shines through a sheet of falling rain, it is very apt to form a rainbow. The same effect is caused, now and then, by moonlight. Even strong electric lights shining through rain and mist have caused this phenomenon.

There is a difference of 65,226 feet—approximately 12.35 miles—between the highest and lowest points on the earth. Mount Everest, the highest peak, rises 29,028 feet. The Mariana Trench in the Pacific, the lowest point on earth, is 36,198 feet below sea level.

The avocado has three singular features: (1) its protein content is greater than that of any other fruit; (2) its ripeness can be determined only by a laboratory test of its oil content; and (3) its growth is sometimes so prolific that trees have collapsed under the weight of their fruit.

The letter used most in the English language is *e*, followed by *t*, *a*, *i*, *s*, *o*, *n*, *h*, *r*, and *d*, in that order. But the letter *s* begins more English words than any other letter, far surpassing its nearest rival, the letter *c*.

In this century, more than 1,600 people have been publicly whipped in Delaware, where an old law provides this form of outdated punishment for the perpetrators of 24 minor crimes.

Prince Wenzel von Kaunitz-Rietburg, an 18th century Austrian statesman, changed his clothes no less than 30 times daily. This obsession occupied about four hours a day.

The French horn is a brass instrument; the English horn is a woodwind, while the trumpet marine is the name of a stringed instrument, and is not a horn at all.

In 1976, 134,400 arrests were made for vehicle thefts. In the same year, 1,029,300 people were arrested for driving under the influence of alcohol.

The U.S. Patent Office has on file a patent for boots with pockets for use by nudists.

Architecture is often a thankless job. We have no idea today who designed and built many of the most notable structures on earth, including the Taj Mahal, the Pyramid at Giza, and most medieval cathedrals.

The 11th-century Pope Benedict IX was 23 years old when he *died*! He had reigned for 12 years, after becoming pope at the age of 11!

Did you know that when you eat tapioca pudding, you're eating a dish made from the starch of the Brazilian cassava root?

In 17th-century America, "trials by touch" were held in which the defendant in a murder case was forced to touch the body of the victim to see if the corpse "gave a sign." The belief was that if the murderer touched the body of the victim, the corpse would move or somehow indicate the individual's guilt.

To date, we have had only one lefthanded President, James A. Garfield, and even he was subjected to the conversion attempts of his parents. Though eventually he learned how to write with his right hand, he did not abandon the use of his naturally dominant left. Legend has it that our 20th President once demonstrated his ambidextrous powers by writing Latin with one hand while he wrote in Greek with the other.

In 1925, a large crowd filled a hall in New York's Hotel Roosevelt to watch Yale defeat Harvard in the first intercollegiate crossword puzzle tournament.

The Board of Councilmen in Canton, Mississippi, once passed a resolution that stipulated:

"1. We shall build a new jail.

2. The new jail will be built out of the materials of the old jail.

3. The old jail will be used until the new jail is finished."

Sheer Coincidence

In 1925, a staff composer for Witmark, the New York music publisher, wrote a song called "Me Neenyah." The company printed and copyrighted it at once. Soon after, copies were sent to Europe, and a music publisher in Germany informed Witmark that the song was an infringement on one which had been copyrighted in Germany in 1924. Witmark and his composer compared the two pieces and found them identical, note for note, with the exception of one half-tone. Clearly, it was a coincidence—a composer might steal a few bars but not an entire melody. The German publisher and Witmark agreed on this point, and the matter was dropped.

On April 14, 1910, a record 12,226 paid customers attended the opening-day ceremonies of the baseball season in Washington, D.C., and saw President William H. Taft throw out the first ball. Taft was the first President to perform the honored task, and the baseball season has traditionally begun the same way ever since.

Under Cover

The English didn't invent the umbrella, but they did develop the first practical waterproof bumbershoot, late in the 17th century. The man usually credited with popularizing the umbrella in London was one John Hanway, a 17th-century traveler who brought the brolly to England from Portugal. Hanway created quite a stir by strolling through London under the strange contraption in all kinds of weather, and was often greeted by jokes from passersby. He was especially likely to suffer abuse from coachmen, who feared the popularity of such a device would cut into their trade.

Religious Londoners objected to the umbrella on moral grounds—after all, the purpose of heavenly rain was to make people wet. But despite these objections, the use of the umbrella spread steadily in the showery city. For some time, they were called Hanways in honor of their eccentric pioneer.

An annual growth rate in the world's population of just two percent would result in a doubling of the population every 35 years! The present birth rate is about 1.8 percent.

The American President who fathered the greatest number of children was John Tyler. Tyler was the father of 14 children by two marriages. Tyler's immediate predecessor, William Henry Harrison, was the second most fertile father among U.S. Presidents. Harrison had 10 children. Curiously, both Presidents were born in Charles City County, Virginia.

Only four gems are considered precious in today's jewelry market. The four gems are diamond, emerald, corundum in two forms (ruby and sapphire), and chrysoberyl. Pearl, which is an organic substance rather than a mineral, is also considered precious.

During the 19th century, some umbrellas were designed with one protruding side to offer protection for the bustle that most women wore in those days.

West Point, the U.S. Military Academy, was established in 1802, when the academy graduated but two of its 10 students. There are now five military service academies in this country. Besides West Point and the U.S. Naval Academy in Annapolis, Maryland, the other service academies are: the U.S. Air Force Academy, Colorado Springs, Colorado; the U.S. Coast Guard Academy, New London, Connecticut; and the U.S. Merchant Marine Academy, Kings Point, New York.

Delaware was the first state admitted to the Union. The last of the 13 original colonies to be admitted was Rhode Island, which joined on May 29, 1790, over two years after Delaware had ratified the Constitution.

Amor, Amor

John Barrymore was indubitably the most amourous actor in Hollywood. In the title role in the film *Don Juan*, which premiered at Warner's Theatre in New York on August 6, 1926, Barrymore kissed his various leading ladies a total of 191 times in the two hour and 47 minute duration of the picture. That was an average of one kiss every 53 seconds!

Young puffins are fed and fed until they grow larger than their overworked parents. Then their parents fly away. The youngsters are too fat to start food-searching on their own, but well larded as they are, they don't starve. They live off their stored fat, gradually getting thin enough to go out on their own.

Talk about bouncing babies! The heaviest normal newborn infant was a Turkish boy weighing 24 pounds, four ounces, born on June 3, 1961. The lowest birth weight of a surviving baby was a 10-ounce girl. The tiny infant was born in England on June 5, 1938.

Upon assuming the consulship in 60 B.C., one of Julius Caesar's first acts was to establish a daily bulletin of government announcements, the *Acta Diurna,* to post in the forum. Posted proclamations and the announcements of town criers—and the grapevine—provided the news to many city residents for centuries, but it wasn't until the 17th century that newspapers proper began to spring up around Europe on a regular basis.

In the late 17th century, the German monarch Frederick William decided that the potato could solve his nation's food shortage, and decreed that all peasants should plant spuds. Those who refused would have their noses and ears cut off! It's unknown how many farmers lost their facial features because of the bog apple, but Frederick's decree may help explain why potatoes have become so popular in Germany.

Popcorn is actually an Indian invention. The first Americans to enjoy popcorn were the colonists who attended the first Thanksgiving dinner, on February 22, 1630.

He Got It for Peanuts

The first American to be honored by a commemorative statue in India was George Washington Carver, whose numerous discoveries of industrial uses for farm products included a large variety of peanut products. In 1947, five years after Carver's death, the peanut growers of India erected a monument to the black inventor in Bombay. The peanut wizard was also honored by the American Congress, which made Carver's Missouri birthplace a national monument in 1943.

Pierre Auguste Renoir, one of the great masters of the Impressionist school of painting, was partly disabled by arthritis and gout during the later years of his life. Yet he never ceased to paint. During his last years, Renoir often could not hold his paint brushes, and instead had to work with the brushes strapped to his wrist.

Another French artist saw the aged Renoir working one day and asked: "Why do any more? Why torture yourself?"

Renoir's reply was: "The pain passes but the beauty remains."

Three thousand feet below the sea's surface, its waters are pitch black. Not even a tiny bit of the sun's light can penetrate down more than half a mile. Sea creatures that live at depths below 3,000 feet have been found to be blind or to possess their own phosphorescent "lighting system."

Forgetful Fiddler

Trains and cabs must be the greatest repositories for "left objects." Every once in a while something of real value is forgotten by a passenger. Every once in a rarer while, the story has a happy ending.

On February 25, 1979 Alexander Schneider left his violin in a New York taxicab. This extraordinary instrument is a Guarnerius, estimated to be worth $250,000. You can well imagine Mr. Schneider's distress. Picture his glee when the instrument was returned to him. The two men who found it in the cab are band musicians and say they will share the $13,500 reward offered by the insurance company with the other members of their band.

Metric Measure

The two systems of measurement now in use are the Metric and the English system. Oddly enough, the English have recently converted to the metric system.

The meter is defined in terms of light-waves. According to this definition, one meter is equivalent to 1,533,164.12 wave lengths of the red light emitted by cadmium.

If you think Adelle Davis brewed up a storm over nutrition, you should have been around when Sylvester Graham, the father of the graham cracker, was stirring up the country with his lectures and books in the 1830s-1840s. He antagonized thousands by opposing such standard commodities as tea, coffee, tobacco, liquor, meat, corsets, and featherbeds. He also persuaded thousands to follow his diet, which included bread made of coarse flour, since known as Graham flour. The number of Grahamites became so great that, to accommodate them, scores of Graham boarding houses were established, and restaurants set apart special Graham tables.

A flying honeybee beats its wings 250 times a second; the housefly, 190 times a second.

Pool Shark

In 1956, the great pocket billiards champion Willie Mosconi won a tournament match against Jimmy Moore by running the entire game—150 balls—in one inning. Moore played a safety shot on the break, and never got to shoot again.

The skillful Mosconi once ran 526 balls in a row—a world's record—and won the world's championship in 1953 by running the game in only two innings.

The expression "breed like flies" is quite apt. If all the descendants of a single pair of flies survived, they would number over 335 *trillion* at the end of one summer.

A Peasant a Day

Otto of Bavaria went to his grave firmly convinced he'd murdered hundreds of innocent peasants. In 1886, the line of succession to the Bavarian crown left Otto as the nominal king, but the Prince never assumed the throne. He'd been declared insane and locked in a room by his family for the previous 14 years. There the Mad Prince carried on a spirited repartee with the ghosts that lived in his dresser drawer, and indulged a singularly gruesome belief: The murder of a peasant a day would keep the doctor away.

Each day, one of Otto's guards would load the Prince's gun with blanks while another guard donned peasant garb and strolled in a field beside Otto's window. The Prince would appear in the window, take aim, and fire—and the "peasant" would obligingly fall dead at the sound of the shot.

A Fish Story

The largest fish ever caught by any method was a 17-foot-long, 4,500-pound white shark, harpooned by Frank Mundus off Montauk Point, Long Island, New York in 1964.

The largest fish ever caught by rod and reel was a white shark measuring 16 feet 10 inches long and weighing 2,664 pounds. It was brought in by Alf Dean at Denial Bay, near Ceduna, South Australia, on April 21, 1959.

An angry llama will spit in his antagonist's face.

French Cut-Off

Parisian flophouses of the nineteenth century offered their more indigent guests a place at the "two-penny leanover," a long bench with a rope stretched in front of it which the sleeper could lean over during his sit-up slumber. In the morning, an inaptly named "valet" rudely awoke the guests by cutting the rope.

In France, the king's bed, known as the "Bed of State," was treated with a reverence that sometimes surpassed that afforded the throne itself. Persons entering the king's chamber were expected to genuflect in front of the bed, even if the king was not in the room.

In 1195, the Sultan of Marrakesh, Morocco, ordered that 960 sacks of musk be added to the mortar for a minaret he was building to commemorate a military victory. That minaret still stands, and the fragrance of the musk can be perceived today.

A mathematician once computed the number of permutations possible with a standard 11-by-11-square crossword puzzle— that is, given 122 squares and a 26-letter alphabet, how many different puzzles could be constructed? The answer was found to be 24,873 plus 222 zeroes. That's higher than the number of seconds that have elapsed since the beginning of the universe!

To escape its many enemies, a flying fish shoots out of the water and glides as far as 500 feet on its greatly enlarged fins. Some of the most powerful of flying fish can even jump over the deck of a small ship.

In the days of ancient Greece, an hour was defined as one-twelfth of the day. But the day was measured from sunrise to sunset. Thus, the daytime hour was longer in summer than in winter!

The city of Troy described by Homer in *The Iliad* was located not in Greece, but in present-day Turkey. When the supposed site of the ancient city was excavated late in the nineteenth century, nine cities were found, one on top of the other. The sixth city to be built on the site is thought to be Homer's Troy.

For many years, the tobacco habit was bitterly opposed by the English crown and the English church. In his *Counterblast to Tobacco*, King James I described smoking as "a custom loathsome to the eye, hateful to the nose, harmful to the brain, dangerous to the lungs, and in the black stinking fume thereof nearest resembling the horrible Stygian smoke of the pit that is bottomless."

For a few centuries after their invention in the thirteenth century, eyeglasses were regarded as a sign of respect, suggesting learning and importance. Contemporary paintings often depicted saints wearing spectacles. A portrait of St. Jerome, painted in 1480 by Domenico Ghirlandajo, showed a pair of spectacles dangling from the saint's desk, though Jerome died a thousand years earlier. So St. Jerome later became the patron saint of the spectacles maker's guild.

Among the many misconceptions the Greek philosopher Aristotle entertained was the belief that men have more teeth than women. And Aristotle was married twice!

Chinese women, as well as the men, enjoy smoking a pipe. Their pipes are extremely delicate and unusually decorated. Cigarettes, on the other hand, which caught on only in the Chinese metropolises before the advent of Mao, are less common in China today than they were 25 years ago.

Have you ever wondered why the little red schoolhouse was painted red? The custom originated in the Northeastern United States, where red paint was cheaper than any other color.

The hanging Betty lamp was one of the first lighting devices of Pilgrim America. The metal lamp contained a wick set in a slot and a reservoir filled with fish oil. The term Betty owes nothing to a woman of that name—the word was probably derived either from the German *besser,* "better," or the French *petit,* "small."

Although Oslo was the traditional capital of Norway, for many centuries the city was named Christiana. The change was made in 1624, after the original Oslo burned down and was rebuilt, on the opposite side of the Aker River, by King Christian IV. Then, after World War I, Norwegians petitioned their legislature to restore the ancient name of their main city. On July 11, 1924, a law was passed stating, that as of January 1, 1925, the capital would again be called Oslo.

Salmon have leaped as high as six feet in ascending waterfalls. Some species of trout can also swim up waterfalls, against the current.

We all recognize such phrases as *plastered, under the table, soused, tipsy,* and *bombed* as slang synonyms of *drunk,* but many more colorful terms for insobriety have been lost from the language. Of the over 400 terms for inebriation that have been coined since Colonial days, *bungey, nimptopsical, cherry-merry,* and *as stiff as a ringbolt* have all fallen into disuse.

Although the whale weighs over a hundred tons and the mouse tips the scales at only a few ounces, they develop from eggs of approximately the same size.

Still Good!

Prohibition made the sale, manufacture, or transportation of alcoholic beverages illegal in this country. Evidently the news never made it through the bureaucratic labyrinth of Washington, D.C.; for during Prohibition, the U.S. Department of Agriculture continued to distribute pamphlets explaining how to make alcohol from apples, bananas, pumpkins, and other fruits.

The word "daisy" comes from two Anglo-Saxon words meaning "day's eye," since the yellow center of the flower reminded the Anglo-Saxons of the sun. "Dandelion," meanwhile, comes from the French *dent-de-lion*, meaning "tooth of the lion." The French thought the jagged leaves of the flower resembled the teeth of a wild animal.

One Type of Speedster

The record for rapid typing is held by Albert Tagora of Paterson, New Jersey, who on October 23, 1923, typed an average of 147 words a minute for one full hour. During that stretch, Tagora ran off 8,840 words—for an average of 12½ strokes per second!

Just Desserts

The first commercially-made ice cream in the United States was sold by a Mr. Hall in New York City in 1786. The first ice cream soda was reputedly concocted by a Robert Green of Philadelphia, who, in 1874, added ice cream to plain soda water. But credit for the first ice cream cone goes to a young ice cream salesman at the 1904 Louisiana Purchase Exposition in St. Louis—or rather, to his date. The salesman, Charles E. Menches, gave an ice cream sandwich and a bouquet of flowers to the young lady he was escorting, and she rolled one of the layers of the sandwich into a cone to hold the flowers, thus founding an American institution.

Tobias Hobson, an innkeeper in Cambridge, England, under Charles I, is responsible for the term *Hobson's Choice*. When a guest at Hobson's inn asked for a horse, he was escorted to the inn's stable by Hobson himself, who told the traveler that he could choose any horse he wanted—except that he must choose the horse standing nearest the door! So, today, we call a choice that offers no alternative *Hobson's Choice*.

Lobsters reach full maturity after about eight years. An adult lobster usually measures from 12 to 14 inches in length and rarely weighs more than ten pounds. But the largest lobster on record measured three feet from mouth to tail, and tipped the scales at 42 pounds! This giant crustacean is now on exhibit at the Museum of Science in Boston.

The French long considered oysters a brain food. In the 15th century, King Louis XI feted the Sorbonne professors on oysters once each year "lest their scholarship become deficient."

To *put another feather in one's cap* now refers to any creditable exploit or acquired honor. The phrase comes from a custom in ancient Lycia, where a feather was added to the hat of a warrior each time he killed an enemy.

Christians differ widely in their concepts of the afterlife, but the Koran tells Moslems exactly what to expect in Heaven. After a 300-course banquet, the right-living Mohammedan male will be given eternal youth and vitality, and will be presented with a palace, 80,000 servants, and 72 beautiful wives, whose youth and pulchritude will endure forever. Amen.

That the Dutch people were not well-thought of by the English in the 18th century is shown by a number of disparaging phrases—containing the word Dutch—which came into our language under the reign of Charles II. False courage, especially if produced from excessive consumption of alcohol, is called *Dutch courage;* telling a person in distress to remember that things might have been worse is called *Dutch comfort;* a cowardly surrender is called a *Dutch defense;* and an outing on which the invited party must pay his own way is called a *Dutch treat.* Perhaps the most pejorative term is a *Dutch bargain,* a deal made while the buyer is in his cups. The most flattering term is *to talk like a Dutch uncle,* which means to criticize or reprove someone—severely, but kindly.

Girl Scout Troop 12 of Great Falls, Montana is unique in the annals of scouting. Every member of the troop is a grandmother—and the 13 scouts have a total of 119 grandchildren. The youngest member of Troop 12 is 56; the oldest, 90.

Annette van Dorp was a 23-year-old student in Bonn, Germany, when she conceived the idea of how to make some money to pay her way through college. She realized what a chore it was for people to cut and trim large lawns. So she bought some sheep and rented them out for lawn cropping.

Her business thrived—in fact, became so good that now she owns over 100 of these animals. Her clients, residents of the city of Bonn, like the arrangement very much. They say that it costs $15.00 an hour to employ a person with a mowing machine, and that one sheep, at a cost of only $10.00 for the entire summer, will keep something like 150 square yards of grass short and nice.

The leotard, a close-fitting garment worn by dancers, and sometimes by actors and acrobats, is named for its creator, Jules Leotard, a famous French aerialist of the 19th century. Although today the leotard is worn by performers of both sexes, Monsieur Leotard originally designed the costume to enhance male sex appeal. At the close of his memoirs, the celebrated daredevil addressed his masculine readers thus: "Do you want to be adored by the ladies? [Then] put on a more natural garb, which does not hide your best features."

Leotard's leotard was a one-piece elastic garment, with ankle-length tights and no sleeves. Today, the leotard usually covers both arms and legs, although legless and sleeveless varieties are available.

The first portable timepiece was made in Nuremberg in 1504 by Peter Henlein. Because of their shape and heft, these early watches were called "Nuremberg live eggs." The first wrist-watch appeared as early as 1790. It was made by Jacquet-Droz and Leschot of Geneva.

The first metal coins were minted in the kingdom of Lydia, in Asia Minor, around the year 650 B.C., although there is evidence of silver money in Persia as early as 760 B.C.

Around the middle of the 19th century, the bicycle in common use—called a high-wheeler—consisted of an extremely large front wheel turned by the pedals, and a very small rear wheel. Front wheels with 54-inch or even 64-inch diameters were common, while the rear wheel sometimes measured no more than 12 inches across!

The heaviest weight ever lifted by a human being is 6,270 pounds, accomplished by Paul Anderson at Toccoa, Georgia, in 1957. The 5-foot, 10-inch strongman, using his back, lifted a table loaded with a lead-filled safe and heavy auto parts. The weight of the objects equalled that of a 33-man college football team!

On the morning of February 9, 1855, strange hoofprints were seen about in the snow in Devonshire, England. The oval impressions, about the size of donkey hoofprints, were eight inches apart in a straight line, as if the mysterious animal had been walking a tightrope, and covered a distance of 98 miles, passing through 15 towns and a river. But the weirdest thing was that the tracks ran up and down the sides and roofs of barns and houses, continuing on the ground on the other side of these structures. The scientists who examined the tracks claimed they were made by no living creature, and many of the residents of Devon, declaring the abominable snowman must be the Devil himself, refused to leave their houses at night for many months thereafter.

The coffee plant is a tropical evergreen shrub indigenous to the eastern hemisphere; 25 species grow wild in Africa, Asia, and the Near East. Oh, there is some coffee grown in the United States—but only in Hawaii.

Two species of the coffee plant are far and away the most common. *Coffea arabica*, the oldest known variety, hails originally from Arabia or Ethiopia, and is now grown extensively in South America. *Coffea robusta* originated in East and Central Africa and is still the major coffee plant of the continent. *Robusta* is not—well—more "robusta" than *arabica*. Actually, it's milder in taste and aroma, and is less favored by Westerners.

Brazil once accounted for 66 percent of all coffee exports, but as Africa production has continued to rise, that figure has dropped to 40 percent. Today, about 30 percent of all coffee comes from Africa.

Sardanapalus, the last great king of Assyria, had quite a thing for beds, right to the end. According to a Greek tale, the monarch committed suicide, along with his wives and concubines, on a pyre fueled by his 150 beds.

Lightning Strikes Twice?

Contrary to folk wisdom, lightning does strike twice in the same place, and may even strike as many as ten times in a single spot! Successive photographs of lightning flashes have been taken by engineers of the General Electric Company during electrical storms in the Berkshire Mountains of Massachusetts.

One can get an appreciable shock from an ordinary electric socket in a house wired at a voltage of 115. A single flash of lightning has been estimated to carry a charge of 100 million volts.

Elektro, the mechanical man, was made by the Westinghouse Company, and first exhibited in New York City during the World's Fair of 1939-40. The seven-foot, 260-pound robot was set in motion by vibrations of the human voice. He could walk, smoke, count on his fingers up to 10, tell whether an object held before him was red or green, and perform 20 or so other feats. Elektro's electrical system contained 24,900 miles of wire, or enough to encircle the globe.

About 19 percent of all the paper manufactured in the United States is made from wastepaper. In West Germany, where the supply of pulpwood is more limited, 45 percent of all paper is made from waste; in forest-rich Finland, only three percent.

The idea of identifying the various throws of the dice with names such as *snake eyes* and *boxcars* is hardly new. The ancient Greeks also had names for the dice throws. A six was known as *Aphrodite,* and a one was called a *dog.*

Altar Addicts

The most-married man in history has got to be King Mongut of Siam, on whose life the book and movie *The King and I* were based. Mongut had 9,000 wives and concubines. Other spectacular polygamists include King Solomon, with 700 wives, and Queen Kahena of the Bergers, with 400 husbands.

Anyone can swim or float more eaily in salt water than in fresh water because salt water is heavier, and thus has greater buoyancy. There is so much salt in the Great Salt Lake of Utah, that one cannot sink or completely submerge oneself in it. Nevertheless, an inexperienced swimmer can drown if he panics and loses his balance. Although his body will float on the surface, the brine will suffocate him.

Pin $

For centuries, metal pins were rare and costly items reserved for the rich. You've heard the expression *pin money*, meaning a small sum allotted by a husband for his wife's use, or money for incidental expenses. Well, when the term originated in the 14th century, *pin money* was just that, for at the time, pins were expensive enough to be real items in the budget. By custom, a husband would present his wife on the first or second of January with enough money to buy her pins for the year.

Pin money went by the boards in the 19th century, when mass production made pins the inexpensive purchase they are today.

During the World War I, German and Austrian submarines were called *Untersee Boats*, or undersea boats, and were designated by *U* followed by a number. Eventually, all submarines came to be known as U-boats.

If the air-conditioning were turned off in the Houston Astrodome, the entrance of warm humid air could cause it to rain in the stadium.

Charles Steinmetz, the electrical wizard, was an inveterate smoker. Although a notice forbidding smoking was posted in the General Electric plant where Steinmetz worked, the great man ignored it until one day an executive asked him rather pointedly if he was not aware of the rule. Steinmetz answered with a cold stare.

The next day, Steinmetz didn't show up for work; and for two days thereafter, no one heard from him. The laboratory of the General Electric plant was practically at a standstill. Without Steinmetz, they just couldn't go ahead.

So the management ordered that a serious search be made throughout the city to locate their genius. After a while, they found him in the lobby of a Buffalo hotel. He was seated in a huge chair, puffing away nonchalantly at a huge cigar. When he was told that the whole company was out looking for him, and was asked why he had, without so much as a goodbye, left his office without notice, he calmly replied, "Well, I just came up here to have a good smoke."

After that, there was never a word mentioned to him about the no smoking rule.

The monkey wrench does not owe its name to our endearing fellow-primate. Rather, the term is a corruption of Moncke wrench, after a London blacksmith, Charles Moncke, who invented the implement.

The original peeping Tom was the only man to view the naked Lady Godiva on her famous ride. The legend of Lady Godiva is that her husband, Leofric, Lord of Coventry, imposed steep taxes on his subjects, which led his wife to protest against the hardship. Leofric met Godiva's complaints with the answer that he would remit the harsh taxes only if she would ride naked through the town.

The charitable beauty issued a proclamation explaining the purpose of her riding in the raw, and requesting all the townspeople to remain indoors with their shutters closed during the performance. The good lady's appeal was honored by everyone except Tom the tailor, who bore a hole in his shutter in order to get a glimpse of the naked woman. Tradition has it that Tom was struck blind for his impertinence. In any case, Lord Leofric did rescind the burdensome taxes.

The Orient has produced many picturesque names for more mundanely-titled Western inventions. For instance, the Chinese for *locomotive* is *fire wagon*; for *telephone, electricity talk*; for *safety razor, gentleman instrument*; for *movie theater, electricity shadow hall*; and for *life insurance, man old-age guarantee to feel at ease*.

Ulysses S. Grant was actually christened Hiram Ulysses Grant. The name change occurred when the Congressman who nominated Grant for West Point erroneously wrote the youth's name as Ulysses Simpson Grant on the application form. Simpson was the maiden name of Grant's mother. The young cadet took advantage of the error as an excuse to get rid of the name Hiram, which he considered too old-fashioned.

An irreverent wag has pointed out that two drinks are mentioned in the Bible—Wine: *which gladdeneth the heart of man*, and Water: *which quencheth the thirst of the jackasses*.

New pinball games are being invented continually. Each of the four major pinball machine manufacturers now brings out from six to 12 new games every year. Designers say they aim for a game that demands about 75 percent skill, but allows for 25 percent luck so that unskilled players can enjoy playing as well.

How many drops are there in a pint? Well, there are two cups in a pint, and eight ounces in a cup. An ounce contains two tablespoons, and a tablespoon is equal to three teaspoons. Finally, a teaspoon contains 120 drops. So one pint contains 11,520 drops.

Steam Heat

Automobile enthusiasts were aghast. The world's speed record was held, not by one of their pet gasoline-powered cars, but by an automobile with a steam engine in its nose. And the honor of being first to travel faster than two miles a minute had gone to this traitorous device.

It happened in January, 1906, when the Frenchman Marriott took his steam-powered Stanley to Daytona Beach, Florida. On the sands outside Ormond, Marriott sped over a measured mile at a rate of 121.52 miles per hour!

Not until 1908 did the gasoline engine return unto its own. Then a huge Fiat named *Mephistopheles* zoomed to a new record, searing the cinders at the rate of 121.64 m.p.h.

The youngest player ever to don a major-league baseball uniform was Joe Nuxhall of the Cincinnati Reds. Nuxhall was a tender 15 years, ten months when he suffered a six-run, one-inning shellacking at the hands of the St. Louis Cardinals on June 10, 1944.

Many Americans caught their first glimpse of the banana at the 1876 Centennial Exposition in Philadelphia. The fruit sold there for ten cents apiece, a high price at the time. Despite the banana's skin, each was wrapped in tin foil. Bananas were still unfamiliar to most Americans that the fruit and the telephone became the two most curious items at the Exposition!

Aspirin is today the most widely used medicinal drug in the world. Americans alone swallow about 22 billion tablets each year—close to 100 pills annually for each person!

The world's largest rodent is the capybara, also called the carpincho or water hog. A native of tropical South America, it can attain a length of 3½ to 4½ feet and a weight of 150 pounds.

The Niftiest Natator

When Johnny Weissmuller retired from amateur competition in 1929, he could have taught Tarzan himself how to swim.

The handsome swimmer won his first National Championship in 1921. From then on, Johnny made records in every free-style distance from 100 yards to 880 yards and even held the world's record for the 150-yard backstroke.

His mark of 51 seconds flat for the 100 yards stayed on the record books for 17 years!

The face is sometimes dubbed the *mug* owing to the 18th-century practice of carving grotesque human faces on the outside of drinking mugs.

Of all symbols appearing on the flags of the world, the star is by far the most common. Forty-one flags have this symbol in one form or another. The second most popular symbol, the crescent, appears on only nine flags.

Captain Allardyce Barclay of Ury, Scotland, once walked 1,000 miles in 1,000 hours to settle a bet.

The average Englishman enjoys 2,000 cups of tea each year—that's almost six cups per day!

There is one family of birds whose young can fly immediately after being hatched. These birds are the mound builders, natives of Australia and some South Sea Islands, which emerge from the shell fully feathered.

Is a Spice an Herb?

What is a spice? According to Christopher Morley, *spice* might be the plural of "spouse." According to Webster, a spice is an aromatic vegetable such as pepper, cinnamon, nutmeg, mace, allspice, ginger, cloves, or such, used to season food and to flavor sauces and pickles.

An herb, on the other hand, is defined as "a seed plant which does not develop a woody tissue as that of a shrub or tree, but is more or less soft or succulent." An herb may be used for medicinal purposes; or because of its scent or flavor, for culinary purposes.

There is but a thin line of distinction between an herb and a spice.

In ancient times, spices were used for incense, for embalming preservatives, as ointments, as perfumes, as antidotes against poisons, as cosmetics, and for medicinal use.

A Carload of Firsts

Gottlieb Daimler, a compatriot of Carl Benz, independently arrived at his own version of the internal-combustion engine that Benz had developed. Although the two never met, the firms which succeeded their enterprises merged and formed the present Mercedes-Benz company.

Perhaps the first truly practical gasoline-powered automobile was the Panhard, designed, in 1894, by a Frenchman named Krebs. The French had begun to produce autos a few years earlier, after Levassor purchased the French rights to Daimler's engine of 1887.

In the United States, several inventors get high marks for pioneering efforts in the field. Among them were the Duryea brothers, who won the first automobile race in America in 1895. One year earlier, an American named Elwood Haynes had gained the patent for a gasoline-powered car that was developed at the Apperson wagon works in Kokomo, Indiana. The first car manufactured in Detroit was made by Charles King in 1896. By 1898, there were no fewer than 50 automobile manufacturers in the United States.

A crossword addict made up what he termed was the largest crossword puzzle in history to be published. It consisted of 25,000 squares, and almost 8,000 definitions. The constructor, Henri Blaise, admitted that his puzzle took him eight years to construct. He estimated it would take the average crossword worker somewhere between three and four months to complete.

The puzzle won't be that easy to market, for it measures no less than three feet in one dimension, and five-and-one-half feet in the other. Furthermore, the definitions fill a book of 170 pages.

A Los Angeles man, named Robert Stil-

genbauer, once compiled, but did not pub-
lish, a crossword with 3,149 clues across and
3,185 clues down. Stilgenbauer sent out
125,000 copies of the puzzle—which required
11 years to compile—but none was returned
correctly completed.

The word "uncopyrightable" contains 15 letters, none of which is used more than once.
And the nine-letter word "strengths" contains
but one vowel.

A Gem of a Bet

Among the cleverest historical wagers was
that made by Cleopatra of Egypt, with her
lover Marc Antony. The crafty "serpent of the
Nile" bet the Roman general that she could
drink 10 million sistertia ($500,000) worth of
wine before leaving the table. Antony rose to
the bait, losing the wager when Cleopatra
dropped two pearls, valued at the agreed-
upon sum, into a glass of wine, which she
then drained.

A Most Unusual Escape

In 1899, Pearl Hart became a folk hero when she and an accomplice robbed one of the last Western stagecoaches. Sentenced to five years in prison for her part in the crime, Pearl was isolated from the men prisoners in the Yuma, Arizona, jail for fear she'd "corrupt their morals."

But after six months in jail, Pearl appeared to turn over a new leaf. She began reading books and writing poetry. The warden and the prison chaplain visited her often in her cell, and the governor himself once came to Yuma to see the "new" Pearl Hart.

One day, Pearl began complaining of illness. A nurse examined the jail's only woman inmate, and declared her pregnant. The warden was aghast. There were only two keys to Pearl's cell: his own and his wife's. Only two other men had ever been alone with Pearl in her cell: the prison chaplain and the governor of the Arizona Territory.

Pearl was conditionally pardoned in 1902 because of a "lack of accommodations for women prisoners."

Among other nicknames, New York City is sometimes known as "Gotham." Washington Irving first used the term, around 1805, to refer to "The Big Apple," since the residents of Gotham, England, were long regarded as fools.

But there is another side to the story. The residents of Gotham, England, were said by some to have purposefully played the fool in order to discourage royal visits. In that way they would avoid the expense of entertaining the king. An old saying from the English town goes something like this: "More fools pass through Gotham than remain in it."

A Kentucky law still on the books makes it illegal for a married man to buy a hat unless his wife is along to assist in the selection.

In 1914, as the United States prepared to open the Panama Canal, Secretary of State William Jennings Bryan sent invitations to the opening to the navies of a number of countries, including Switzerland. A land-locked nation, Switzerland never had a navy.

Mercury, the planet closest to the sun, is thought, by most people, to be extremely hot. Actually, at all times half of the planet is extraordinarily cold, with temperatures in the neighborhood of -250 degrees. The side of Mercury facing the sun, however, is broiling hot—temperatures there approach 700 degrees.

If all space between atomic particles were eliminated, matter in the resultant state—called the neutron state—would be so dense that one cubic inch would weigh about 1,800 million tons.

The comic character Superman made his first appearance in June, 1938, in one of four stories presented in *Action Comics*, Number One. A copy of this comic is now valued by collectors at over $4,000!

Superman merited his own comic book in the summer of the following year. A copy of *Superman* Number One is now worth over $2,000.

The Millionaire Racehorse

The greatest racehorse in American history was undoubtedly Man o' War. Bought at auction for $5,000 in 1918, the phenomenal speedster went on to win 20 of the 21 races in which he was entered, earning close to $2,000,000 in purses and stud fees. So certain was Man o' War's victory, that on some occasions the odds in his favor approached 1-to-100!

In addition to his race-course earnings, the remarkable stud sired 383 sons and daughters, who won a total of $3,500,000 in purses.

Man o' War was the first animal whose obituary and biography appeared in the list of celebrities compiled by the major press associations. The horse also had the largest personal guest book on record, with the names of 2,000,000 people who visited him in retirement. When Man o' War died in 1947, his funeral was attended by 2,500 admirers.

The longest recorded drive of a badminton bird is 79 feet, 8½ inches, achieved by Frank Rugani in California on February 29, 1964.

The creature with the longest recorded life span is—no, not the tortoise or parrot—but the lake sturgeon. One of these fish reportedly attained the age of 152 years!

Coffee became widely popular in London during the 17th century. The first coffee house opened its doors in 1652. Soon coffee houses became the centers of political, social, literary, and business life in the city. In America, the first popular coffee houses opened as early as the 1680s—and the *Mayflower* listed among its cargo a mortar and pestle to be used for grinding coffee beans.

In 1965, a New Zealand resident produced the longest loaf of bread ever baked—20 feet, 5 inches long. The loaf weighed 50 pounds.

Tommy Woods, working for his college's radio station in Wayne, New Jersey, disc-jockeyed for 272 hours without a break in 1972—that's 11 full days!

A Close Shave

Peter the Great, Czar of Russia from 1682 until 1725, wanted his countrymen to adopt Western customs and dress. To discourage the growth of beards, which were then unfashionable in Europe, the Czar first levied a tax on all beards, and later decreed that men wearing beards would be shaved by force with a blunt razor, or would have their whiskers removed one by one with a set of pincers. On one occasion, Peter personally cut off the beards of his noblemen.

In 1975, voters in Philadelphia reelected Francis O'Donnell to the City Council. By election day, O'Donnell had been dead almost a week, but election officials had not had time to remove his name from the voting machines.

A recent survey revealed that more than half of all adults in France have not read a single book since childhood.

The members of some insect species are so short-lived that they have no way of eating Some completely lack a mouth!

The social weaver bird of Africa really deserves its name. As many as 90 couples may join to build a huge community nest. A favorite location is a big acacia tree. After the nest is built, each pair of weavers goes to work fashioning its own individual chamber inside the large structure—a bird version of the modern apartment house.

Jackhammer Blues

Even the largest, most well-equipped symphony orchestra in the world could not perform John Cage's *First Construction in Metal* without first scouting around for a number of additional instruments. The score for this avant-garde piece calls for, among other things, a piano with a metal rod strung across the strings, 12 oxen bells, eight cow bells, four brake drums, five thunder sheets, four Turkish cymbals, four Chinese cymbals, three Japanese temple gongs, tubular bells, sleigh bells, a tom-tom, and—from the blacksmith's shop—four muted anvils.

Word Play

Is a *skilligalee* something you might cook in, or a bacteria that causes a common disease? Would you buy *calibogus* in the lumberyard, or in a department store? Even if you're a crossword puzzle aficionado, these unusual English words may have you stumped. The answer to both questions is: neither. *Skilligalee* is a kind of soup, although you'd probably never come across any, as it's given mainly to sailors or prisoners; *calibogus* is a concoction made of spruce beer and rum.

Want some more? What's a *cothamore?* A *jobbernowl? Rumblegumption?* (Answers: an Irish overcoat; a dunce; a Scottish word for common sense.)

The longest and heaviest of all snakes is the anaconda of South America. Specimens have been reliably reported to be as heavy as 950 pounds, and as long as 37½ feet.

The world's record for non-stop see-sawing is 101 hours, set by two California boys in 1964.

A statue in the plaza of Guayaquil, Ecuador, bears the name of José Olmedo, that nation's most famous poet. But the figure is actually a representation of Lord Byron, bought by the Ecuadorians in a London junk shop to save money.

The Dry Liquid

Liquid and *wet* are virtually synonymous, but in fact not all liquids are wet. At room temperature, mercury runs like water and changes its shape according to the container in which it is placed, making it a bona fide liquid. But mercury will not wet your fingers when you touch it.

The first air-conditioned office building in the United States was the Milam building in San Antonio, Texas, which was completed in 1928. The 21-story structure was the first office building in the world to be built with air-conditioning as a part of the original construction.

The flying squirrel does not have wings, and, strictly speaking, it cannot fly but only glides from tree to tree. No mammal except the bat is capable of true flight.

King Richard II of England was so careless with royal funds that the monarch once had to pawn his crown to make ends meet.

The Statue of Liberty in New York City was paid for by donations from French citizens. American donations paid only for the concrete pedestal of the statue.

The longest shadow on earth is believed to be the one cast by El Pitron Peak on Tenerife, one of the Canary Islands. The mountain rises 12,200 feet above the Atlantic Ocean, and at sunrise and sunset casts a shadow nearly 150 miles long.

The Geodesic Dome is the only man-made object that becomes structurally stronger as it increases in size.

French artist Paul Cezanne, much noted for his still lifes, worked so slowly at his craft that he often had to use wax fruit as still life models. Real fruit would have rotted before Cezanne could finish his painting.

Americans are the most avid bowlers on earth—an estimated 65 million people bowl in this country. But the largest bowling alley in the world is to be found, surprisingly, in Japan. The Tokyo World Lanes Bowling Center boasts 252 lanes.

A Deadly Device

The mace is a shafted weapon held in one hand. It employs a flail at the end of a chain. The flail, or spiked ball, is linked to a wooden handle by the chain. While it cannot be snapped like a whip, the mace is wielded in much the same fashion. It was possible to envelop the opponent's sword blade with the chain, and thus to pull his weapon from his hand, or to knock the enemy senseless within his armor with the mace. One could even crush his skull.

In England, this weapon was called a *Morning Star*. In Spain, it was called a *mate suegra* or "mother-in-law killer." Originally a farmer's thresher, the mace became, as so many tools did, a peasant's weapon. Spikes were added to the ball to make it more effective. The length of chain made it easier to swing it about, and clear a path through a wall of armor.

If you're traveling in Europe, don't ask an Albanian for directions to Albania. The name of that nation in its native tongue is Shqiperia.

What do the words *millinery*, *palace*, *meander*, and *tawdry* have in common? They all owe their origin to a place name.

Women's hats of striking beauty were made in the city of Milan, Italy; *millinery* became the word for women's hats. Wealthy Romans built large, luxurious homes, or *palaces*, on the Palatine Hill in Rome. In ancient Greece, a winding, wandering river was called the Menderes, which spawned the word *meander*. And St. Audrey's fair in Norwich, England, became famous for the cheap, low-quality jewelry that was sold there. *Tawdry* now describes any cheap, shoddy goods.

It's commonly believed that the city of Rome was founded by the Etruscans, and that the language the Etruscans spoke formed the basis of Latin. Actually, the Etruscans warred continually with other peoples on the Italian peninsula, and were more often an enemy than an ally of the early Romans.

The Etruscan language, meanwhile, is totally unrelated to Latin—unrelated, in fact, to any other known language. Even today it remains only partly deciphered. And no one is sure where the Etruscans lived before they reached Italy.

The smallest of all birds is the bee hummingbird which is about 2¼" long, most of that length being the beak. It takes 18 of these creatures to tip the scale of one ounce.

It is commonly thought that an intestinal parasite, like a tapeworm, produces an insatiable appetite in its host. Actually, the amount of food necessary to maintain a parasite of this type is almost infinitesimal.

There is a source of light energy right here on earth that is far more powerful than the sun. A laser beam, produced by energizing an artificial ruby in a certain way, emits the equivalent of 10,000 watts of light energy per square centimeter. The light energy emitted by our sun over the same area is six watts.

The body of the average adult contains 2,800 square inches of skin, making the skin the largest single organ in the human body.

What does it mean when the weatherman says that one inch of rain fell in your area yesterday? For instance—say one inch of rain fell on one acre of ground. Since an acre equals 43,560 square feet, a rainfall of one inch over this area would produce 6,272,640 cubic inches of water, or 3,630 cubic feet of water. A cubic foot of water weighs about 62.4 pounds, the exact weight varying with the water's density. Therefore, one inch of rain over one acre of surface would equal 226,512 pounds, or better than 113 tons of liquid.

It has been calculated that in the last 3,500 years there have been only 230 years of peace throughout the civilized world.

A Bolt from the Blue

The intense heat of lightning is sometimes responsible for odd accidents. One lady's earring was melted by lightning, and another bolt soldered all the links in a one-yard chain. The U.S. National Safety Council's Report for 1943 told of a soldier being welded into his sleeping bag when the zipper was struck by lightning. The startled soldier had to be cut loose.

The most famous of all golf courses and clubs is the Royal and Ancient of St. Andrews. Founded in 1774, its basic rules were soon accepted throughout the world. After 1888, the year when the St. Andrews Golf Club of Westchester County, New York, was founded, the game gained in popularity in the United States.

Nicotine Nostalgia

Originally, tobacco derived almost exclusively from Turkey. American cigarette manufacturing dates from the Civil War period. During that era, Greek and Turkish tobacconists in New York City hand-rolled the expensive tobaccos then popular among the carriage trade: Havana, Turkish, Perique, Cavendish, Persian, Cut Navy, Latakia, and St. James. By the 1880s, natural leaf cigarettes, such as Bull Durham, began to dominate the market. The hoi polloi could buy a pack of smokes for a nickel.

Fatima, Sweet Caporal, Vanity Fair, Between the Acts, Melachrino, Murad, Wings, Spud—do these names ring a bell? Well, some of them are still around, but most of them are only nostalgic memories to veteran smokers.

What really revolutionized weaponry was the invention of gunpowder, usually attributed to the Chinese firecracker-makers of the 9th century. Gunpowder was introduced into Europe in the 1300s. Field artillery and cannons were first used by the Dutch.

The first advertised radio broadcast was transmitted from Brant Rock, Massachusetts, on Christmas Eve of 1906 by Professor Reginald Aubrey Fessenden. But the first radio station with a regular broadcasting schedule—KDKA of Pittsburgh, Pennsylvania—did not come on the scene until 1920. Today, there are more than 4,370 AM stations and 2,350 FM stations broadcasting in the United States.

In medieval France, King Philip Augustus decreed that the points on his subjects' shoes should be between six and twelve inches, depending upon their station—the longer the point, the higher the rank.

Speed Demon—
19th-Century Style

Chicagoans were out in force on Thanksgiving Day, 1895. They came to see a new-fangled contraption called an automobile. A few of the gasoline-powered horseless carriages were going to race.

The route lay from the heart of Chicago to a nearby suburb and back. The road measured exactly 54.36 miles. The winner would have to cover that terrific distance without breaking down.

J. Frank Duryea busted the tape seven hours and 17 minutes after the start of the race. He had covered the distance at an average speed of 7.5 miles an hour!

The crowd went wild!

The Miracle, one of the most spectacular dramas ever presented in the United States, required a cast of 700 and a theatre redesigned to resemble a Gothic Cathedral. When the play went on the road, a train of 204 cars was needed to transport the actors and equipment.

George Washington was the father of our country, but he was not, strictly speaking, the first American president. That honor belongs to John Hanson of Maryland, who was chosen *President of the United States in Congress Assembled* in 1781, before the executive branch of government had been established as a separate entity by the Constitution. Hanson was succeeded in the post by Elias Boudnot, Thomas Mifflin, Richard Henry Lee, Nathan Gorhan, Arthur St. Clair, and Cyrus Griffin. So, George Washington, the first chief executive elected under our present Constitution, was actually the eighth president of the United States.

Unconscious Hostility Par Excellence

The newspaper Vecerny Pravda, reported that Vera Czermak jumped out of her third story window when she learned her husband had betrayed her. Mrs. Czermak recovered in the hospital after landing on her husband, who was killed.

The loveable koala bear is a finicky eater. He'll touch nothing but eucalyptus leaves.

The first widely-known professional basketball team was the Original Celtics, founded in 1915 by a group of New York City youngsters. The squad disbanded in 1928, then regrouped in the 1930s as the New York Celtics, before permanently disbanding in 1936. At the height of their popularity, the Celtics played a game every night and two on Sunday, and were almost continually on the road. Yet during the 1922-1923 season, the Celtics amassed a whopping 204 wins against just 11 defeats!

The first neon-tube advertising sign in the United States was installed in 1923, on marquee of the Cosmopolitan Theater in New York. The sign beckoned playgoers to a production of *Little Old New York*.

When chocolate first reached Europe in the 16th century, the clergy declared it "the beverage of Satan" and "a provocative of immorality," since it was thought that chocolate was an aphrodisiac. The idea did not die easily. As late as 1712, the English magazine *The Spectator* warned that men "be careful how they meddle with romance, chocolate, novels, and the like inflamers."

Until the 19th century, most paper was made from substances derived from old linen and cotton rags, or from straw. Then papermakers found out how to make paper from wood pulp. At last there was an inexpensive, seemingly inexhaustible supply of raw material for paper—and the forest fire became the single most dangerous threat to world literacy.

Figure skating was first included in the Olympic Games in 1908, reappeared in 1920, and became part of the Winter Games when they were instituted four years later. Norwegian Sonja Henie was the most noted figure skater of that period, winning the Norwegian championships at age nine, and the world title at age 13! She captured gold medals at the Winter Olympics in 1928, 1932, and 1936, then went to Hollywood to star in a number of movies. Among other innovations, Sonja was the first woman skater to wear the short skating skirt.

Among the many activites that kept the prolific Thomas Jefferson busy, was the compilation of a unique Bible. About 1804, during his first term as president, Jefferson put together a 46-page New Testament, consisting of excerpts from the four gospels, arranged according to a scheme of Jefferson's own invention. *The Jefferson Bible*, composed primarily of Jesus' actual words, was originally intended to teach Christianity to the Indians. But Jefferson was so pleased with the work that he used the book for his own bedtime reading.

When Bobby Fischer threw a tantrum in Reykjavik, and then arrogantly ceded two games to Spassky before his blew Boris off the board, he performed a commercial alchemy. Thousands of chess books that had been gathering dust in the publishers' bins for many years suddenly became prime property, and chess sets—old or new—were transmitted overnight into pure gold.

The boom is still on, and the variety of chess sets is still proliferating. Today, the game—who'd have thunk it?—is the rage of cops, hardhats, and John Wayne.

Tests have been conducted to determine the more humane way to prepare a lobster for human consumption. In the test, one lobster was plunged alive into boiling water, while another was submerged in cold water that was then slowly brought to a boil. The lobster plunged rudely into boiling water perished within a minute, squeaking and moving about the pot in apparent pain. But the second lobster remained quite passive as the water heated up, eventually swooning and passing on gracefully—without squawking.

The tests are of interest to the diner as well as to the lobster, for lobsters boiled slowly were found to have tenderer, tastier flesh than those put to a speedy death.

The first pencil factory in America was established in Concord, Massachusetts, in 1812, when William Monroe made 30 cedar pencils and sold them to a Boston hardware dealer.

But it was in the City of Brotherly Love that the first American pencil with an eraser was produced. In 1858, Philadelphian Hyman Lipman was granted a patent for a pencil with a piece of rubber glued into a groove at the end.

Billionaire Howard Hughes designed a bed for himself which was equipped with piped-in music and hot and cold running water! It employed 30 electric motors to move himself and various parts of the bed!

In 1840, English cheese makers probably thought they'd established the all-time record for cheese size when they delivered a half-ton Cheddar as a bridal gift for Queen Victoria. Little did they suspect that, 124 years later, the Wisconsin Cheese Foundation would produce a mammoth Cheddar tipping the scales at 34,591 pounds! The Cheddar was delivered for exhibition at the 1964 World's Fair in New York City aboard a specially designed, 45-foot-long refrigerated trailer called the "Cheese-Mobile."

There are presently an estimated 363 million television sets in use throughout the world, with the United States the leader by far with 120 million receivers, Japan 25 million, and England 18 million. And yes, there are still some countries that have no television at all.

Backgammon is the oldest board game still played today. Archaeologists, excavating the ancient Sumerian city of Ur, found five game boards in the royal cemetery that bore a resemblance to backgammon boards. The 5,000-year-old Sumerian game was played on a board of 20 squares, with six dice and seven pieces for each player.

Women's basketball has been around since the 1890's, when Clara Baer introduced the game at a New Orleans college, using the rules published by basketball inventor James A. Naismith. But Clara misinterpreted some of Naismith's diagrams, assuming that certain dotted lines Naismith had drawn, to indicate the best area for team play, were actually restraining lines to be drawn on the court. Thus, for many years, women's basketball was played under different rules than the men's game, with each player limited to movement only within certain parts of the court.

Today, the women's game is played under the same rules as the men's games, and the former women's game is called "rover" or "netball."

In 1955, the General Electric Company reported that scientists in their laboratories had succeeded in manufacturing a synthetic diamond by subjecting carbonaceous material to pressures of one-and-a-half million pounds per square inch, and temperatures over 5,000 degrees. The synthetic diamonds, the largest of which was a mere one-tenth of a carat, were of industrial quality only.

Mozart's piano pieces, as well as Beethoven's first piano sonatas, were composed for pianos with only five octaves.

Phantom of the Opera and other works may have contributed to the popular misconception that the city of Paris is built over a vast maze of ancient sewers and catacombs. While it is true that a network of caverns lies under Paris, these caverns are neither ancient nor catacombs. Most of the present sewer system was constructed during the mid-19th century, by Georges Haussmann. The older caverns were not used for burial until 1787, and prior to that were actually stone quarries.

Fifteenth-century Chinese scholars compiled an encyclopedia consisting of over 11,000 volumes.

During the Renaissance, cheese eating fell out of fashion among the upper classes in Europe, partly as a result of the warnings of physicians that it was an unhealthy, undigestible food. A writer of the time named Thomas Muffet wrote that cheese "lieth long in the stomach undigested, procureth thirst, maketh a stinking breath and a scurvy skin."

John Kemble, a noted English actor of the early nineteenth century, devised a rather ingenious method for erasing a debt. Saddled with a bill for room and board that he could not pay, the actor spun a top around his room over the head of his sick landlord. Much to Kemble's delight, he was promptly evicted.

Talk about slow basketball games! Until 1937, the referee had to throw up a jump ball after every basket!

The rarest and most valuable button in the world is the "Morse" or "Cope" button, a magnificent work of art fashioned by Benvenuto Cellini in 1530 for Pope Clement VI. A large, round, and flat button measuring six inches in diameter, it is made of gold and encrusted with gems. Over the beautiful diamond at the center is an image of God the Father. According to his *Autobiography*, Cellini worked 18 months on this one button and employed a staff of 10 artisans to help him.

Kleenex tissues were originally manufactured as gas mask filters during World War I.

A Costly Comma

In 1872, Congress passed and the President signed a Tariff Act listing among non-taxable items "fruit-plants, tropical and semi-tropical for the purpose of propagation and cultivation. . ." At least, that's what the lawmakers *thought* the law read. Actually, a typist had inadvertently inserted a comma instead of a hyphen after "fruit," with the result that "fruit, plants, tropical and semi-tropical. . ." became exempt from import taxes instead of the intended "fruit-plants."

A harmless error? Keen-eyed lawyers spotted the mistake, sued the Treasury Department for tariff refunds in behalf of a group of fruit importers, and won over $3,000,000 as a settlement. The attorneys then used the cash to finance the construction of the Culver Line railroad in Brooklyn, New York, that later became part of New York City's rapid transit system. Thus, a misplaced comma financed a railroad!

If upon their arrival in Bethlehem the Three Wise Men had invested one dollar at four percent interest, their account would now be worth a quantity of gold 100,000 times the size of the earth!

Here's one for Western fans: a 10-gallon hat actually holds ¾ of a gallon.

The keenest sense of smell exhibited in all nature is that of the male silkworm moth. It can detect the sex signals of a female 6.8 miles away!

Fishy Business

Try as you might, you won't find the word *sardine* on any list of fish species, for strictly speaking, there is no such thing as a sardine. What we eat as sardines are actually any of a number of small, thin-boned fish, usually herring or pilchards, that are suitable for packing in oil. Conceivably, a can of sardines may contain fish of a number of different species.

The first attempt to devise a "Tilt" mechanism for pinball machines was crude indeed. Nails were hammered into the underside of the machines to provide a painful surprise to players attempting to slap the board from underneath.

From India, nutmegs and cloves, native to the Moluccas—the Spice Islands—were introduced into China. A tradition has come down to us that in the 3rd century B.C., the courtiers of the royal court were required to carry cloves in their mouths in order to sweeten their breath when addressing the emperor.

The literary achievements of English poet Percy Bysshe Shelley seem all the more remarkable when you remember that the poet died at the age of 29. And Shelley's contemporary, the poet John Keats, died a year before Shelley—at the age of 25!

Pianoforte comes from two Italian words: *piano* which means soft, and *forte* which means loud. So pianoforte actually means "soft-loud." The piano, which is what most of us call a pianoforte, was the first keyboard instrument ever invented which could play both soft and loud.

Time on My Hands!

Have you ever wondered what kind of individual spends his time toiling over the construction of crossword puzzles? Well, of 100 regular contributors to two New York puzzle magazines, 25 are currently in prison.

About one-third of the 18 million volumes in the Library of Congress, the world's largest book and manuscript depository, are too brittle to be handled.

The bidet, that peculiarly Gallic instrument for feminine hygiene, made its first appearance during the early eighteenth century. The device, first mentioned in 1710, must have been unfamiliar to many Frenchmen in 1739, when a dealer offered a bidet as a "porcelain violin-case with four legs."

The Ritz Carlton Hotel in New York was originally equipped with bidets, but the hotel was forced to remove them after a flood of complaints from outraged Puritanical guests.

The easternmost part of Brazil is actually half the distance from Africa as it is from the United States. Traveling due north from Natal, Brazil, you would reach a point in the North Atlantic Ocean only a few hundred miles west of the Azores—far closer to Europe than to North America!

Have you ever tried to figure out what bodies of water the expression *seven seas* refers to? Don't waste your time. The *seven seas* is a figurative term meaning all the waters of the earth. The expression appears in the ancient literature of the Hindus, Chinese, and Persians, as well as in Western cultures.

When in 1608, Thomas Coryat, an Englishman who had visited Italy, introduced the Italian custom of eating with a dinner fork, everyone thought the idea was an insult to human dignity. But little by little, of course, this affront became standard practice.

In September, 1938, a tremendous hurricane struck New England and parts of Long Island, killing 600 people, destroying 275 million trees, downing 20,000 miles of electric wires, damaging 26,000 automobiles, and demolishing hundreds of homes. Near Madison, Connecticut, a two-story house was blown a half-mile by the storm and came to rest *upside down*. Oddly enough, not a single window pane was broken!

Al Capone's business card described him as a "secondhand furniture dealer." Capone grossed about $105 million in 1927.

The 18th-century Italian Cardinal Mezzofanti spoke 53 languages fluently, another 61 tongues almost as well, and understood 72 more dialects, for a total of 186 languages and dialects. Yet the Cardinal never left Italy in his entire life.

Sic Transit Records

Helene Madison held 16 swimming records at one time. At the end of 1932, the 6-foot, 18-year-old blonde from Seattle, Washington, held every important free-style swimming record. She had smothered all Olympic competition.

She was the first woman to swim 100 yards in one minute flat. Tank experts predicted that her records would last for generations. Today, not a single one of Helene's marks stands.

Shake, Rattle, and Roll

There's a certain art in even such a seemingly simple activity as shaking fruit from a tree. In general, a hard, slow shake is preferable to a quick, short motion. But for each fruit there's a specific frequency that's best. Plums, for example, will fall about three times as freely if the plum tree is shaken 400 times a minute, two inches per shake, than they would at 1,100 times a minute, one inch per shake. Cherries respond most favorably to 1,200 short shakes per minute, while apple trees are most generous when shaken 400 times per minute.

Diamonds Are Forever?

Whether true beauty lies without or within, a jewel is a rare and a precious thing. The most precious stone today is the ruby, which after 1955 became increasingly rare as supplies from Ceylon and Burma dwindled. Carat for carat (one carat equals 200 milligrams), a flawless natural ruby of good color is more valuable than a diamond. An excellent six-carat ruby, for instance, recently brought $30,000 on the open market.

If rubies have topped diamonds in the gem hierarchy, diamonds nevertheless remain a girl's best friend. The diamond is the most durable of all gems—90 times harder than the next hardest mineral, corundum. Commercially, the diamond is used to cut other stones.

If heated sufficiently, diamonds will burn. Although an ordinary fire will not ignite them, a blow torch will do the job easily. Diamonds are not affected until the temperature reaches from 1,400 to 1,607 degrees Fahrenheit, depending on the diamond's hardness. Such high temperatures are not common in ordinary fires, but they were achieved in the great 1906 fire which destroyed San Francisco.

In an average year in the United States, one teenage girl in every 50 gives birth to an illegitimate child. About half of the over 400,000 illegitimate children born in this country each year are born to girls age 15 to 19, including over 10,000 born to girls under 15 years old.

Women 40 years of age or older give birth to about 2,300 illegitimate children each year.

A titmouse is not a mouse, but a small bird. A ladybird is not a bird, but a beetle. A silverfish is not a fish, but an insect. And a guinea pig is not a pig, but a rodent—and it doesn't come from Guinea, either!

The parents of the famous sculptor, Sir Jacob Epstein, were religious people. His mother, who took the religious injunction "Thou shalt not create graven images" quite seriously, dumped a pile of her young son's works into the trash can. These would have been worth a pretty penny today.

Our number system uses a set of numerals commonly referred to in the West as "Arabic numerals." These numbers were devised not by the Arabs, but by scholars in India. It was the Arabs, however, who introduced the numbers to Europe.

Astronomers have estimated that stars range in size from bodies 2,000 times as large as the sun to others as small as the moon.

There is no "weather" in the stratosphere. This region of the atmosphere, which begins about six miles above the earth, is above the clouds and the weather changes we experience occur only below. Blizzards and rainstorms do not occur in the stratosphere, where it is still, quiet, and bitterly cold—often more than 100 degrees below zero!

The Vatican Library contains writing materials from pre-Columbian Peru and Mexico that were made from human skin.

George Washington had no children. His wife bore four children during her earlier marriage to Daniel Custis, two of whom died in infancy. Only one of the other two children lived long enough to have children of his own.

Incidentally, when George Washington married Martha, she was considered to be the richest widow in Virginia, having inherited an estate of 17,000 acres from Custis, along with 300 slaves. Washington himself had 49 slaves when he married.

Don't bother looking for a rainbow during the next noontime sun shower. A rainbow can be seen only in the morning, late afternoon, or night, when the sun is at a certain distance above the horizon.

In regard to the world fuel supply, the birth of an American child has the same effect as the birth of eight children anywhere else in the world. For the average American uses eight times as much fuel energy as the average person outside of the United States.

Laconic—or pithy—speech, originated in Laconia, the ancient Greek country of which Sparta (Lacedaemon) was the capital. The Laconians were famous for their economical way with words. Julius Caesar's *Veni, vidi, vici* ("I came, I saw, I overcame") is classic laconic speech. But even terser was the reply sent by the Spartans to Philip of Macedon, who boasted, "If I enter Laconia, I will level Lacedaemon to the ground." The Laconic response was one word: *If*.

The largest shark in the world, the *Rhincodon typus*, or whale shark, can grow to a length of 50 feet, and specimens 70 feet long have been reported. But there's no need to fear the jaws of this mammoth creature—the whale shark eats plankton.

The first explosion of an atomic bomb took place on July 16, 1945, in a desert area near Alamogordo, New Mexico. This was only 21 days before a similar device was detonated over Hiroshima, Japan.

The banana, whose prevalence in Central America has given rise to the phrase "Banana Republic," is actually a native of Asia.

In the early 1950s, an estimated one-quarter of all the males in Tibet were Buddhist monks.

Double Your Pleasure

Norman L. Manley stepped to the seventh tee at the Del Valle Country Club course at Saugus, California. The date was September 2, 1964. He hit a prodigious drive, and the ball bounced unerringly to the green and into the cup. He had scored an ace, one of the longest ones on record. But the best was yet to come. On the very next hole, the 290-yard eighth, Manley, bubbling with excitement and confidence, hit another mammoth drive. As if directed by radar, that ball landed smack in the hole! Manley had hit two holes-in-one, back to back, scoring six strokes under par for the pair.

The highest tides anywhere in the world are to be found in the Bay of Fundy, which separates New Brunswick from Nova Scotia. At the head of the bay, a few times each year, the tides rush in and out at a rate of 10 feet an hour—an incredible 60 feet from highest to lowest tide. The tide moves nearly as fast as the water rises in a bathtub with both taps opened full, and the rise of the tide goes on for six hours, twice a day. At no time is the water in the bay still.

A seven-inch North African ostrich egg takes 40 minutes to boil.

Botanists in the seventeenth century were fascinated by a strange fungal growth that much resembles a small bird's nest with a clutch of tiny eggs. This fungus, *Cyathus striatus*, was thought by some to actually contain eggs. Others thought the egglike lumps inside the cup of the plant were seeds. Still others claimed to have seen these lumps give birth to live birds!

Of course, none of these claims were true. The spongy lumps within the acorn-sized cups are actually spore sacs, filled with thousands of tiny spores. The plant's resemblance to a bird's nest appears to be completely incidental: the fungus derives no benefit from its inadvertent mimicry.

The Hindus of India are said to play more varieties of musical instruments than are found in all other countries combined. The Hindus have several thousand instruments, for virtually all of their early instruments remain in use. In fact, their most popular instrument is still the seven-stringed vina, which was invented more than 1,200 years ago.

A Bird's-eye View

The bird on the wing is a symbol of man's aspiration to be more than man, to soar above the natural world. The combination of grace and power epitomized by a bird in flight is both nature's pride and man's joy.

The bird's evolutionary progenitor was the reptile, and several birds—such as the ostrich, the penguin, and the kiwi—remain bound to earth. As the bird moved up the evolutionary scale, it developed many fantastic traits. For example, a bird can focus its eyes more quickly than any other living creature. Its sight is astonishingly keen; so is its sense of hearing; its smell, however, is poor.

For the tea ships of 1610, sailing from the Orient to Europe was perilous. The seas swarmed with pirates and cutthroats; there were few charts to show reefs and rocks; and the frail vessels were often sunk by storms. In 1618, another method of transportation was tried—tea was brought by camel caravan from China across the deserts and mountains of Asia to Eastern Europe. The journey took 18 months.

A marble slab used as a game board in the early days of Christian Rome bears a cross and the inscription: "Christ grants aid and victory to dicers if they write His Name when they roll. Amen."

In 1817, an Englishman named Ashford accused a gentleman of murdering Ashford's sister. The accused, Thornton, challenged Ashford to decide the case in battle, and appeared in full armor, with a lance and a sword, to settle the matter. Ashford, naturally, did not appear for the combat.

Thornton then claimed he had won the case—and he was right. Parliament had neglected to officially abolish the medieval custom of trial by battle!

The word "idiot," far from a complimentary term today, is derived from a Greek word that originally meant merely a private citizen or layman. Thus, all men not in public office were "idiots." Today, we tend to regard the converse as more apt.

The world's largest gem reposes not in a wealthy dowager's vault but in a glass case on the fifth floor of the American Museum of Natural History in New York City. A topaz of 1.38 million carats, taken from Brazil's Minas Geraes, it weighs 596 pounds. It is rather dull-looking, and few of the visitors who make it up to the fifth floor pay this huge gem any mind.

Before a baby bird is hatched, it has a temporary tooth that enables it to break out of the egg. Full grown, a bird may have a beak strong enough to crack seeds, or long enough to snap up little creatures from the bottom of a stream.

For almost 200 years, a festival called the Fiesta of the Radishes has been held each December 23 in Oaxaca, Mexico. During the festival, immense radishes are sold, and native artists carve them into many shapes—fantastic figures of men and animals. Prizes are awarded for the best and most imaginative shapes.

Cheers!

The Italians are currently the reigning world champions in the per capita consumption of wine. The average Italian consumes about 30 gallons of *vino* each year, about three gallons more than his French counterpart. Portugal ranks third in wine drinking, at about 21 gallons per person, while Argentina and Spain round out the top five.

The people of the Soviet Union apparently enjoy making wine far more than they do drinking it. The U.S.S.R. ranks fourth in wine production after France, Italy, and Spain, though it places a mere 19th among wine consumers. The United States, which ranks a distant 31st in wine consumption at just 1.7 gallons per person, nevertheless stands as the sixth leading wine producer, with Argentina number five.

Americans do somewhat better at beer consumption—the 21-gallon per person annual figure makes the United States the 13th leading consumer of the foamy brew. Czechoslovakia is the leader at about 40 gallons per person yearly, while West Germany and Australia follow. But in beer production, the United States is far and away number one. American breweries turn out close to four-and-a-half billion gallons each year, almost double the figure for the second-ranking nation, West Germany.

At the other end of the scale, the people of Iceland and Israel rank as the premier teetotalers among all alcohol-consuming nations.

The Sears, Roebuck Company is the largest retailing company in the United States. In 1973, Sears totaled over $10 billion in sales—almost twice as much as its nearest competitor for top honors, the Atlantic and Pacific Tea Company (A & P).

Well over a thousand persons each day commit suicide worldwide, including about 70 Americans. Hungary can—well, boast the highest annual rate, about 37 suicides per 100,000 persons.

Firearms and explosives rank first overall as the preferred method of suicide in the United States, followed closely by poisoning. Poisoning is the preferred method worldwide, though hanging, strangulation, and suffocation rank first among males.

Barnum's Biggest Star

In 1882, Jumbo—the largest elephant ever seen in captivity—was sold by the London Zoo to P.T. Barnum. A loud cry of protest immediately arose from the elephant's English admirers—who included Queen Victoria in their numbers. But the protest was to no avail—the elephant sailed to America with a deluge of gifts sent by his English friends. The gargantuan pachyderm—to which we owe the term "jumbo"—was part of Barnum's circus until the elephant was killed by an express train in Canada in 1885.

Protective Custody

A hornbill must find just the right size hole in a tree for a nest. The female slips inside and there lays her eggs.

The male seals off the entrance with mud, leaving only a narrow slit. Inside, the female is both protected and imprisoned while incubating her eggs. She gets food from her mate by sticking her bill out of the slit. When the young are full grown, the seal is broken, and the young leave the home with their mother.

Shampoo, which to us means to wash your hair, comes from the Hindu word *shampu*, which means to press. A good shampoo is one where you press your fingers hard against your scalp, so our word still indicates part of the original Hindu meaning.

Livy relates that when the barbarians overran the Golden City, a Roman senator sat still, unmoved at everything, until a Goth touched his beard—then he struck, although he died for the blow.

Adolf Keifer won more than 2,000 swimming races. He won his first U.S. championship in 1935, when he was 16 years old. For eight years thereafter, the great backstroker was undefeated, and won 24 indoor and outdoor championships.

In 1946, at the time of his retirement from amateur competition, Keifer held every backstroke record in the books. In a brilliant athletic career, Keifer had lost only two races out of more than 2,000!

The grebe, the mute swan, some ducks, and the loon have a special way of caring for their young. Very often, especially at the first sign of danger, the crested grebe sinks until its back is level with the surface of the water. Its young climb onto its back. Then the parent grebe rises to its swimming position, and with strong strokes carries them across the water to safety.

The Bill for Biking

The most important bicycle race in the world today is the annual Tour de France. Begun in 1903, the race is now one of Europe's major sporting events. Originally 3,560 miles long, the present course stretches about 2,780 miles through France, Spain, Switzerland, Italy, and Belgium. An estimated 15 million people in France alone turn out to watch the bikers as they wend their way over hill and dale and climb over mountain passes as high as 8,000 feet. In some towns, petty criminals are released from jail for the day so that they can take in the spectacle.

One observer has calculated that if one-third of all Frenchmen lose one-third of a day's work due to the race, the Tour de France takes a toll of close to two billion dollars on the French economy!

In 1935, the Illinois State Legislature passed a bill designating "the American language" as the official tongue of that state. "English" was outlawed.

Smoking Out the Smokers

These days, pipes, cigars, and cigarillos are taking an increasing share of the tobacco sales, while the popularity of non-filter cigarettes has declined precipitously in recent years. Yet the Surgeon General's report on the hazards of smoking has hardly meant the last gasp for filtered cigarettes. More filtered cigarettes are now sold each year than the year before. Demon nicotine seems to have secured a niche in the American way of life.

And, by the way, it was Europe—not the United States—that developed the filter cigarette. America only lays claim to the invention of the smoker's cough.

The term *drawing room* has nothing to do with sketching. The word *drawing* is actually a shortening of *withdrawing*—for this was the room to which guests "withdrew."

The largest crabs in the world—which live off the coast of Japan—stand three feet high and often weigh as much as 30 pounds.

If you tried to pay the month's rent or your bus fare with cigarettes, people would laugh at you. But in pre-Revolutionary America, tobacco was acceptable legal tender in several Southern colonies. Virginia even enacted a law that taxes should be payed in tobacco.

Snow is not frozen rain. Snowflakes change directly from water vapor into snow, without going through an intermediary stage as rain.

An ostrich cannot fly, but the 400-pound bird can outrun many racehorses.

At the entrance to some bridges you might see the notice: "Break Step." What does it mean? It's a warning that soldiers crossing the bridge should not march in step.

If the vibrations caused by a marching troop happened to equal the "natural period of vibration" of the bridge, the repeated force of the marching steps could build up and cause the bridge to sway and shatter. Thus, a bridge that could easily support the weight of a thousand soldiers might well collapse if the men marched in step.

Wheel 'em Away!

In 1975, two men held up a doughnut shop in Sepulveda, California, and made off with $125 aboard most unusual vehicles—skateboards!

Until the mid-19th century, postage fees in most of Europe and in the United States were paid by the addressee rather than the sender. Junk mail was presumably no problem at the time.

When George Washington Carver began his work with the peanut in the 1890s, the goober was not even recognized as a crop in this country. By 1940, the peanut was the sixth leading crop in America, and the largest crop in the South after cotton.

To build up a market for peanuts, Carver developed no fewer than 301 separate products from the peanut plant, including twine, dye, oil, cheese, ink, soap, and cosmetics. And in his spare time, Carver found over 100 uses for the sweet potato!

A Colorful Tune

Green with Envy, Purple with Passion, White with Anger, Scarlet with Fever, What Were You Doing in Her Arms Last Night Blues is the title—the longest known title to date—of a tune written by Phillip Springer and Nita Jones in 1961.

A tornado that struck St. Louis in 1927 caused $26 million worth of damage in five minutes.

The time required for the earth to orbit the sun—that is, the length of an earth year—increases by about .04 seconds each century.

Georgia, with an area of 58,073 square miles, most nearly approaches the average size of the 48 conterminous states.

Good Things
Come in Small Packages

Mrs. Pemberton, a 16th-century painting by Hans Holbein, brought $30,000 in a 1935 auction. The round portrait is only two inches in diameter.

The Egyptian Queen Cleopatra was Greek by ancestry and had not a drop of Egyptian blood in her veins. The famed Queen of the Nile was descended from a line of brother-sister marriages, and she herself married two of her own brothers.

Between dawn and dusk an acre of peas can increase in weight by 50 percent, owing to the vegetable's high rate of absorption.

Brandy is obtained from wine or the fermented mash of fruit. It is made from grapes, or cherries, or apples, or plums, or apricots, or peaches, or blackberries.

Of the more than 500 elephants that have been exhibited in the United States, only six are known to have been conceived and born here.

As many as 1,652 languages and dialects are spoken by India's 600 million people. Hindi, the official language, is spoken by only 35 percent of the population.

The most common surname in the United States is Smith. Close to 2.5 million Smiths reside here, half a million more than those with the second most common name, Johnson.

About 70 people are shot to death with a handgun in the United States *each day!* About 75 percent of these shootings take place between family members or close friends.

Pinball Wizard

In these days when golfers, tennis players, and other sportsmen are bringing home huge checks for tournament victories, can pinball players be far behind? The first annual Maryland Pinball Championship, held in June, 1979, drew 25,000 participants to more than 100 tournament locations throughout the state. Winners in various categories shared a

$25,000 purse, and the top finisher also brought home his choice of any pinball game used in the tournament. Gary Wease, a 26-year-old sales manager, was crowned Grand Pinball Wizard for his victory in the Class A finals.

There's more to come, too. Promoters of the tourney are now thinking about a Mid-Atlantic tournament in the near future, set at up to 500 locations around the world.

There's been no peace for the residents of Aurora, Texas since April 19, 1897. On that day, a cigar-shaped vehicle, believed to be a ship from outer space, crashed through the window of Judge J.S. Proctor, killing its only passenger. The extra-terrestial visitor—if such he was—was given a Christian burial in the cemetery at Aurora, but ever since, U.F.O. watchers have been besieging the small cow-community of 273 inhabitants with demands that the body of the outerspaceman be exhumed for examination. Unfortunately, the mysterious visitor's grave-marker was stolen a few years ago, and now no one knows exactly were to dig.

John Heidegger, master of the king's revels in 18th-century England, was reputedly the ugliest man of his day—and was proud of the fact. Weary of Heidegger's boasts, British statesman Lord Chesterfield declared that he had seen many a visage more hideous than Heidegger's. The Swiss-born impressario promptly disputed Chesterfield's claim, and the upshot was a 50-guinea wager that Chesterfield could not produce, within a week, anyone uglier than Heidegger.

The English nobleman set out for the seamier sections of London, and there he found a woman whose grotesque features delighted his eyes. Chesterfield escorted the loathly lady in triumph to his friends. But Heidegger, refusing to yield the palm of repulsiveness, removed the hag's hat and set it on his own head. The woman took one look at the wearer of her hat and nearly swooned—so Heidegger won the wager.

The longest street in the world that runs through the same city is Figueroa Street, in Los Angeles, which runs north and south through the city for a distance of 30 miles.

The first Sunday Schools had nothing to do with the propogation of religious teachings, and were, in fact, frowned on by many religious denominations as a desecration of the Sabbath. In 1780, in the slums of Gloucester, England, classes were held on Sunday to teach the three Rs to illiterate child laborers, who worked the other six days of the week from sunup to sundown. Because the classes were held on the Sabbath, the schools came to be known as Sunday Schools.

Until the early 1930s, the natives of a community on the Danish island of Jutland always bowed before a white wall outside the door of their church when entering or leaving the house of worship. Questioned as to the reason for their homage to the blank wall, the Jutland worshipers were unable to give the cause. A historian from Copenhagen made an investigation, and discovered, under the wall's coats of paint, a picture of the Virgin Mary, painted over during the 16th century Reformation as idolotrous. Thus; for four centuries, custom alone had been responsible for the parishoners' genuflections to the wall.

There are over 20,000 slot machines in the casinos of Las Vegas, Nevada—and in the city's supermarkets, drugstores, liquor stores, and restaurants. The average resident of the city spends about $800 a year in gambling casinos.

Tilt!

On June 19, 1939, the city of Atlanta enacted the first pinball legislation in the United States. The bill prohibited the use of the machines and provided for a $20 fine and a 30-day work sentence for violators.

A Journey to Dreamland

Dreams are similar to hallucinations in that they are not usually caused by sense impressions. To be sure, a toothache or indigestion may affect the form of the dream, but it will not determine the content of the dream. While the duration of a dream is a matter of dispute among scientists, many believe that even the most image-crowded dream lasts but a few seconds. All dreams occur in living color.

What gives the dream its restorative power? Little is known for certain about the dream world, but Freud believed that dreams provide a safety valve for suppressed desires, and that dreams actually protect sleep by draining off the emotional turmoil that would otherwise cause a person to wake up.

So many of us have so much trouble getting to sleep in the first place that nearly half a billion dollars are spent annually in the United States on sleeping pills.

An Apollo spacecraft develops more power on lift-off than all the automobiles in England put together.

Double Trouble

In September, 1951, the people of Bermuda were bracing for a powerful hurricane. As the storm swept to within ten miles of Bermuda's coast, winds bent the island's palm trees to the ground. Large-scale devastation seemed certain.

Then, weather bureau observers realized that there was not one, but two storms approaching the island. An even bigger hurricane was coming up right behind the first. The island appeared doomed.

And then it happened. For the first time in recorded weather bureau history, one storm caught up with another and smashed it. The force of the collision weakened both hurricanes and threw them off course. The storms swerved away from the island and blew out to sea, where they wasted their force on the empty ocean.

Bermuda had been saved from one hurricane by another!

In case you've forgotten: Snow White's seven dwarf friends were named Dopey, Grumpy, Sleepy, Happy, Bashful, Sneezy, and Doc.

In the 19th century, students at Cambridge University, England, were not permitted to keep a dog in their rooms. Lord Byron, the famed poet, complied with the rule—he kept a bear instead.

The first building erected by the American Government in Washington, D.C. was the Executive Mansion, designed by James Hoban and modeled after the palace of the Duke of Leinster in Ireland. Construction began in 1792, and the building was first occupied by President John Adams in 1800. The mansion was burned by the British in 1814, but later restored, with all stones painted white to obliterate evidence of the blaze. Since that time, the building has been known as the White House.

Rag Apple, a Holstein bull belonging to the New York Artificial Breeders Cooperative, is said to have sired over 15,000 offspring in the three years and four months of his service— an average of 87 a week.

An apocryphal tale traces the origin of billiards in England to a 16th-century London pawnbroker named William Kew. The Englishman allegedly took down the three balls identifying his pawnbroker's shop and used a yardstick to push the balls around in the street. Eventually, young canons from nearby St. Paul's Cathedral joined in the game. *Bill's yard-stick* became *billiard stick*, and later, billiard *cue*, from Kew. Of course, the clergymen invented the *cannon* shot.

The first house numbers appeared in 1463, on the Pont Notre-Dame in Paris.

Jealous Genius

Michelangelo—the great Renaissance painter, sculptor, architect, and poet—signed only one of his many works: the *Pieta* in St. Peter's. The artist chiseled his name and birthplace on the figure of Mary after hearing a group of sightseers erroneously attribute the work to another sculptor.

People begin to shrink after the age of 30.

Modern Monickers

If you're thumbing through an old book and come across a reference to a city or nation that you've never heard of, the chances are good that you've merely stumbled onto the old name for a well-known place. Among the more recent place-name changes are:

Old	New
Ceylon	Sri Lanka
Siam	Thailand
Mesopotamia	Iraq
Persia	Iran
Ciudad Trujillo	Santo Domingo
Christiana	Oslo
Stalingrad	Volgograd
St. Petersburg	Leningrad
Gold Coast	Ghana
Belgian Congo	Zaire
Tanganyika	Tanzania
Constantinople	Istanbul
Peiping	Peking
East Pakistan	Bangladesh
Northern Rhodesia	Zambia
Danzig	Gdansk

Cocoa and chocolate are virtually unknown as a popular food outside Europe and the United States. Just five nations—the United States, England, West Germany, the Netherlands, and France—now account for four-fifths of all world chocolate imports, and ten nations account for over 95 percent of chocolate consumption.

In 1877, a Dodge county, Wisconsin, cheesemaker named John Jossi set out to make Limburger cheese and instead ended up with a savory, semisoft product we now call Brick cheese. Brick cheese and Liederkranz cheese are the only cheeses invented by Americans.

The word "clam" is actually a generic term used to designate some 12,000 species of bivalves. In Scotland, the word refers to the scallop. In the United States, "clam" usually refers to the quahog, or hard-shelled clam, and the steamer, or soft-shelled clam, though the two sea creatures belong to two entirely different genera of bivalves.

Mangia! Mangia!

Lest anyone doubt that Americans are, on the whole, well fed, the U.S. Department of Agriculture has published statistics on the amount of food we consume in a year. The average American gulps down 1,154 pounds of vegetables, 1,136 pounds of dairy food, 694 pounds of meat and fish, 598 pounds of fruit, and 34 pounds of poultry—for a whopping total of two-and-a-half tons of food per person annually.

The word *bride* is derived from an ancient Teutonic word meaning "to cook."

Culture Vultures

Whether it's the impact of *Live from Lincoln Center* and *Masterpiece Theater*, or something else, Americans are going in for high culture as never before. In 1977-1978, a record 112 million Americans turned out for live cultural performances—62 million to the theater, 25 million to symphony concerts, 15 million to the ballet, and 10 million to the opera. Compare this figure to the audience of 70 million for professional sports events: 39 million to baseball games, 11 million to football games, 10 million to basketball games, and nine million to hockey games.

Ah! Le Fromage!

The French are the world's greatest cheese eaters. Although the United States is the world's biggest cheese producer, the average American consumes from ten to 12 pounds of cheese annually, including about four pounds of cottage cheese. The average Frenchman, on the other hand, consumes some 30 pounds of *fromage* each year.

The backgammon craze is certainly not new. During the Third Crusade in the 12th century, backgammon-like games were so popular among the Crusaders that kings Richard I of England and Philip II of France issued a joint edict prohibiting all gambling games among their troops.

The greatest enemy of the banana is the wind. Due to the weak, leafy stem of the banana plant, winds of just 20 to 30 miles per hour can devastate an entire banana plantation in minutes.

James A. Naismith, the inventor of basketball, originally planned to use square boxes as his targets. When square boxes were unavailable, Naismith substituted two half-bushel peach baskets, and the new game immediately became known as basketball.

The nations of Iceland, Costa Rica, and Liechtenstein have no armed forces.

Skateboard Surge

Skateboards first reached the public eye in 1962, when the proprietors of the Val Surf Shop in North Hollywood, California, began attaching roller skate wheel trucks to boards. But in the mid-1960s, cities from San Diego, California, to Providence, Rhode Island, began to outlaw skateboards on public streets. The bans were due mainly to the loud noise made by the clay composition wheels, and the dangers posed by the boards to the skateboarder himself.

Then in 1973, a California surfer, named Frank Nasworthy, devised the first skateboard with urethane wheels, which provided more traction and a quieter ride than the earlier wheels. Skateboarding soon became safe and acceptable, and the sport took off again.

The first black baseball player to make the major leagues was Jackie Robinson, who made his debut for the Brooklyn Dodgers on April 11, 1947. Seven years later, the first team on which the majority of players were black took the field for the Dodgers. The players were Robinson, Don Newcombe, Jim Gilliam, Sandy Amoros, and Roy Campanella.

The earliest known treatise on medicine was a 2700 B.C. Chinese work entitled *The Classic Herbal*.

Eyeglasses are considered so vital today that it's hard to imagine a world without them. Yet eyeglasses were not commonplace anywhere in the world until about 450 years ago. And precision, individualized lenses date back no further than the 18th century!

Private Words

Medieval monks usually referred to the latrine with the euphemism *necessarium*. But the most common name for the latrine during the Middle Ages was *garderobe*, or *wardrobe*, a term euphemistically comparable to the modern *rest room, water closet, comfort station*, or *john*.

The word *john* probably comes form an older term for the latrine, *jakes*, which in turn, may be derived from the common French name Jacques. The word *privy*, of course, comes from "private." Even our word *toilet* is a euphemism, adapted from the French *toilette*, a woman's dressing table or room, in turn derived from *toile*, a kind of cloth.

The term *passing the buck* came to us from gamblers' argot. In certain card games, a marker is placed on the table before the player whose turn as dealer will come on the next round. This marker, called the *buck*, is passed among the players with the rotation of the deal.

In 1941, the Federal government forced the National Broadcasting Company (NBC) to divest itself of one of its two component networks. One of the networks was sold to Edward Noble, of Life-Saver candy fame, and went on to become the American Broadcasting Company (ABC). The network that Noble purchased for $8 million now boasts an annual TV advertising volume of well over a half-*billion* dollars!

Save Your Pennies!

Norman Rondeau, of Pawtucket, Rhode Island, bought himself a new car for pennies. For 433,000 pennies, that is, tied up in 86 sacks weighing a ton-and-a-half, which Mr. Rondeau delivered to his local car dealer in a pick-up truck.

The largest stone of true gem quality ever exploited was a Brazilian aquamarine that tipped the scales at 229 pounds. Found in 1910, the hefty stone yielded over 200,000 carats of quality aquamarines!

Leafing Through History

Although it was Sir Walter Raleigh who smoked a bowl of tobacco before the Queen and was promptly rewarded with a dousing by a member of the court who thought Walter was burning, it was the Spanish explorers who discovered the Aztecs smoking crushed tobacco leaves in corn husks some 100 years earlier. Cigarette smoking spread rapidly to Spain, with the beggars of Seville getting credit for the first paper-wrapped variety.

Smoking didn't become popular in Northern Europe until the 1850s, when British soldiers brought Russian cigarettes back from the Crimean War. At the same time, cigarette manufacture and tobacco cultivation spread to the United States, where machinery was developed to replace the tedious hand-rolled technique.

Bats are not blind, but their vision is extremely poor. These winged mammals actually fly by radar, emitting high-pitched sounds from their throats and picking up the echoes with their super-sensitive ears.

In Illinois in 1954, copies of Hans Christian Andersen's *Wonder Stories* were stamped "For Adult Readers" to prevent children from obtaining "smut." And in 1876, Mark Twain's *The Adventures of Tom Sawyer* were excluded from the children's room in the Brooklyn Public Library.

To settle an oft-heard dispute: no, the sweet potato and the yam are not the same vegetable. The yam is, in fact, almost never seen in this country—no matter what food packagers claim to the countrary!

Sidney Bechet was the first man to play a number of musical instruments in recording a song. He used six in making *The Sheik of Araby*, released in 1941. The feat was accomplished by recording the first instrument, re-recording it while the second was played in the studio, and so on until the disc contained the parts of all six instruments—soprano sax, clarinet, tenor sax, piano, bass fiddle, and drums.

The General Was a Lady!

One of the most astonishing cases of successful masquerade on record was the woman who rose to the rank of inspector surgeon general of the British army disguised as a man. The woman, who called herself "Dr. James Barry," and was probably the first woman to attend the University of Edinburgh Medical School, served as a colonial medical inspector in South Africa and elsewhere in the British Empire for over 40 years. Dr. Barry was not suspected of being a woman until her death, in 1865. Then, a charwoman called in to lay out the general's body declared the sex of the corpse as female. Dr. Barry had achieved a reputation of extraordinary surgical skill (she performed one of the first successful Caesarian sections of modern times in 1826), and was also renowned as a duellist.

In 1946, casting for distance, Wilbur Brooks of Indianapolis set his toe in the dirt, took a deep breath, and sent ⅝ of an ounce of bait 427 feet for a world's record. Out Wilbur's way the fish never knew what hit them!

A law in Siena, Italy, forbids a woman named Mary to work as a prostitute.

Through the centuries, man has made a great to-do about his hair. Some of the ancients went to great extremes in caring for their beards. The Lords of Nineveh oiled and curled their beards. The Kings of Persia plaited their hirsutulous draperies with golden thread. Early French kings daintily tied their whiskers with silken ribbons. Even today, the Sikhs of India dye their beards, for it is only a flaming red patch that will establish a Sikh as a man among men.

Chew-Chew

No one knows for sure how many people chew gum, but some 35 billion sticks will find their way into American mouths this year. That's about five billion packets, or 25 packets for each man, woman, and child in the United States. At, say, 10 cents a throw, Americans will spend this year some $500 million on gum. And you thought gum-chewing was on the wane?

By the way, studies have shown that the use of gum rises in periods of social tension, and falls in more tranquil times. For instance, the use of gum in this country soared from a per capita 98 sticks in 1939 to 165 sticks by the early 1950s, duplicating a similar rise during World War I. Today's per capita consumption of chewing gum stands at 175 sticks per year. So, as if you needed any further confirmation, the chewing gum barometer suggests that we once again live in troubled times.

A theatre in Manteca, California, erupted in flames shortly after the end of its feature presentation. The film? *The Towering Inferno.*

The sun gives the sea its blue color. Actually, pure sea water is colorless. The surface water absorbs all but the blue rays of the sun. But the sea reflects back the blue rays to make the ocean traveler think the water itself is blue.

On May 13, 1950, Mrs. Julia St. Clair of Jacksonville, Florida, set out with her son on a leisurely trip to California. There were two things unusual about Mrs. St. Clair's vacation trek, however. First of all, the 49-year-old woman and her son *walked* the 2,500-odd miles to the Golden State, reaching Los Angeles on June 25, 1951, 13 months after leaving Florida. And second, Mrs. St. Clair covered the entire distance *pushing a wheelbar-row*—loaded with 135 pounds of food, clothing, and a cat!

A single galaxy may contain more stars than the number of seconds that have elapsed since animals first appeared on earth.

And the number of galaxies in the universe has been estimated at over ten billion!

To Catch a Thief. . .

The French detective Eugene François Vidocq, who served as the head of Paris' famed *Service de Sûrete*, did not learn about crime and the ways of the underworld in any French police academy. Before becoming the most outstanding sleuth of his time, Vidocq was himself a jailbird. Born in 1775, Vidocq was a soldier, deserter, hardened criminal, master of escapes and disguises, and police spy before moving to the right side of the law.

After serving for 23 years in the *Sûrete*, the famed sleuth was removed as its head in 1832, charged with instigating a crime so that he might gain praise for uncovering it. For the remaining 25 years of his life, Vidocq ran a paper mill, employing ex-criminals for his work force.

The record for non-stop Charleston dancing is 22½ hours, set by 23-year-old John Giola in 1926. But what's that compared to the record set by 35-year-old Cathie Connelly in 1969? Cathie did the twist for 101 consecutive hours—more than four days!

If you're searching for a word that can be typed using only the top row of the letter keyboard, you won't have to look further than *typewriter*.

Productions of Shakespeare's *King Lear* were prohibited in England from 1788 to 1820, in deference to King George III's acknowledged insanity.

In 1949, the hair of Swami Pandarasannadhi of India was reported to be 26 feet in length—the longest human hair on record.

Poor Little Rich Man

In 1885, when James Henry Paine died at the age of 80 in his two-dollars-a-week hovel on Bleecker Street, New York City, his neighbors thought he would be tossed into a pauper's grave. For nearly three years, Paine had been a familiar Greenwich Village figure, foraging through trash cans for food and picking up cigar butts in the street. But it seems that Paine had been a miser whose estate was valued at $391,200.

The earliest prototypes of the bicycle of which we have a record appeared in France and England late in the 18th century. These simple vehicles consisted of two wheels linked by a wooden "backbone" upon which the rider sat, propelling the machine by pushing with his feet against the ground.

But these vehicles were virtually useless until 1816, when Baron von Drais of Karslruhe, Germany, introduced a pivoted front wheel that could be turned by a handle, enabling a rider to steer his "hobby horse" for the first time.

The smallest breed of dog extant is the Chihuahua. At maturity, this Mexican wonder generally weighs somewhere between two and four pounds, but some Chihuahuas tip the scales at no more than a pound.

A tombstone in Florence credits one Armato degli Armati, who died in 1317, as the "inventor of spectacles." But the tombstone has been found to be of relatively recent origin; the claim is a complete fabrication. Historians have tried for centuries to trace the true inventor of eyeglasses, but all we know for certain is that they first appeared in the area of Pisa, in Italy, late in the 1280s.

You might think that commercial air service began with the airplane. But by 1914, the Zeppelin Company was offering the first regularly scheduled air flights between German cities, in rigid-framed, hydrogen-filled airships. Despite the dangerously volatile nature of hydrogen, Zeppelin's airships achieved a remarkable safety record on their commercial flights.

By the end of 1861, the paper dollar issued by the Confederate States of America was worth only 90¢ in gold. By 1863, it was worth but 6¢ in gold.

In 1865, a bushel of potatoes sold in Richmond, Virginia for $100, and a pound of coffee, for $40! But this was actually less than the price of the items in most Northern cities.

The greatest single rainfall fell in the Philippines. In 1911, from July 14 to July 17, the floodgates of heaven opened wide over Baguio, and down gushed a record 88 inches of rain—or more than *seven feet of water!*

If you are too tender-hearted to shoot a deer, you can still find yourself an antler trophy— on the ground. Deer shed their horns once a year, during the breeding season.

Well, chocolate contains drugs. In addition to caffeine, the delectable sweet contains *theobromine,* a mild stimulant.

The term *entangling alliances* was coined by Thomas Jefferson, not as is popularly supposed, by George Washington. In Jefferson's first inaugural address, delivered on March 4, 1801, he said, "Peace, commerce, and honest friendship with all nations—*entangling alliances* with none." However, Jefferson may have been deliberately echoing Washington's farewell speech of September 17, 1796, which concluded, "...Why, by interweaving our dealing with that of any part of Europe, entangle our peace and prosperity in the toils of European ambition, rivalship, interest, humor, or caprice?"

The term *red tape*, as a synonym for bureaucracy, originated in 18th-century England, where official and legal documents were tied up with red tape.

The military custom of sounding taps before bedtime originated in public houses, where a signal known as "taps-up" alerted drinkers that the tap room was about to close for the night.

All in a Day's Work

Despite appearances, bees do not wander aimlessly from flower to flower in search of nectar. Many flowers produce nectar at only certain times of the day, and bees follow a timetable which brings them to the right flower at just the right time. A bee's busy day may begin with a dandelion at nine in the morning, continue with a blue cornflower at eleven o'clock, then a red clover at one o'clock, and a viper at about three—for those are the hours at which each of these flowers is most generous with its nectar.

The largest jigsaw puzzle in the world, made in 1954, measured 15 feet by 10 feet and contained over 10,000 pieces.